PRINCETON STUDIES IN INTERNATIONAL FINANCE
No. 78, May 1995

THE MACROECONOMICS OF EUROPEAN AGRICULTURE

THORVALDUR GYLFASON

INTERNATIONAL FINANCE SECTION
DEPARTMENT OF ECONOMICS
PRINCETON UNIVERSITY
PRINCETON, NEW JERSEY

Library of Congress Cataloging-in-Publication Data

Gylfason, Thorvaldur.
The macroeconomics of European agriculture / Thorvaldur Gylfason.
p. cm. — (Princeton studies in international finance, ISSN 0081-8070 ; no. 78)
Includes bibliographical references.
ISBN 0-88165-250-4 (pbk.) : $11.00
1. Agriculture—Economic aspects—Europe. 2. Produce trade—Europe. 3. Agriculture—Economic aspects. 4. Produce trade. 5. Macroeconomics. I. Title. II. Series.
HD1917.D67 1995
338.1'094—dc20 95-15803
CIP

Printed in the United States of America by Princeton University Printing Services at Princeton, New Jersey

International Standard Serial Number: 0081-8070
International Standard Book Number: 0-88165-250-4
Library of Congress Catalog Card Number: 95-15803

CONTENTS

FIGURES

TABLES

BOXES

1 THE FARM PROBLEM

Should central banks concern themselves with agricultural policies? Does Europe's Common Agricultural Policy (CAP) matter for Central and Eastern Europe? Should ministries of agriculture be abolished, or perhaps be incorporated into ministries of environment or even education and culture?

The answers suggested in this study—yes, yes, and yes—are based on recent empirical evidence on the cost to consumers and taxpayers of agricultural protection in Europe in terms of welfare lost and output foregone. The evidence suggests that farm-trade reform could deliver a substantial supply-side impetus to the European economy and to the world economy as a whole. This conclusion is supported by a simple general-equilibrium analysis that identifies the implicit discrimination involved against manufacturing, trade, and services in Europe; the analysis does not even consider the additional costs imposed on developing countries and the emerging market economies in Central and Eastern Europe by denying them access to the European market for their farm produce. In contrast to short-run partial-equilibrium studies, which have generally indicated deadweight losses from farm support that equal, on average, about 1 percent of gross domestic product (GDP), long-run general-equilibrium considerations suggest losses of about 3 percent of GDP.

This finding has macroeconomic implications. By lowering costs and prices, farm-trade liberalization would facilitate a significant, noninflationary decrease in interest rates and unemployment in Western Europe, thus bringing agricultural policies into the purview of fiscal, monetary, and exchange affairs. Farm-trade reform could also pave the way for export-led growth in Central and Eastern Europe and thus help to bring the former socialist countries into the mainstream of European affairs. Even so, agriculture is not so named for nothing. There may remain an important cultural justification for continuing to

The author is indebted to George Alogoskoufis, Alessandra Casella, Gylfi Th. Gislason, Gene Grossman, Arne Jon Isachsen, D. Gale Johnson, Thorolfur Matthiasson, Marcus Miller, Marian Radetzki, Charles Wyplosz, and an anonymous referee for helpful comments and suggestions. They should not, however, be held responsible in any way for the views expressed in the paper.

support European agriculture from public funds. If so, however, such support needs to be made more effective, more efficient, and probably also more equitable than it is now.

History, Technology, Biology

Around 1870, a century after the industrial revolution began in England, the economies of Europe were still predominantly agricultural. Although the proportion of the economically active population tilling the land in the United Kingdom had decreased to about 15 percent, the industrial revolution had not spread rapidly to the rest of Europe, not even to Ireland next door. In France, farming—including hunting, forestry, and fishing—was still the most common occupation, accounting for about half of total employment.

The 120 years or so that have passed since 1870 have seen a slow but steady continuation of the decline in European farm employment. By 1960, employment in agriculture had decreased to 22 percent of civilian employment in the industrial countries as a group, and by 1990, it was down to 7.5 percent (Table 1, panel 1). The share of value added in agriculture as a percentage of GDP fell correspondingly in the same thirty-year period, from 7 percent to below 3 percent (Table 1, panel 2). This trend continues. Output per worker in agriculture has increased slightly on average relative to GDP per worker in the OECD countries, from 53 to 59 percent between 1960 and 1990 (although these averages conceal substantial differences across countries [Table 1, panel 3]). These figures should not be interpreted as precise indicators of income or productivity differences between agriculture and other activities, however; they do not include nonfarm incomes earned by farm families, and they do not reflect accurately the labor input from part-time farm households (Johnson, 1991, chap. 11).

The dramatic decline of agriculture, once the mainstay of the economies of Europe, is a natural consequence of the interaction between technology and biology. The replacement of animal power by mechanical power on the farms, improved chemical fertilization, and other types of technological progress and modernization have increased labor productivity, reducing the number of farm workers needed to feed a slowly growing population whose biological requirements are confined to a fixed number of calories per person per day. As incomes rise and living standards improve, people generally require more or better housing, cars, and clothing, but their demand for food remains essentially unchanged, in quantity if not in quality.

TABLE 1

EMPLOYMENT AND OUTPUT IN AGRICULTURE IN THE OECD COUNTRIES, 1870-1990

	(1) Share of Agriculture as a Percentage of Total Employment			(2) Share of Value Added in Agriculture as a Percentage of GDP		(3) Output per Worker in Agriculture as a Percentage of GDP per Worker	
Country	1870	1960	1990[a]	1960	1990[a]	1960	1990[a]
Australia	—	11.0	5.6	8.5	8.6	58	81
Austria	65	22.6	7.9	11.1	3.1	49	39
Belgium	44	8.7	2.7	6.5	1.8	75	67
Canada	—	13.2	4.2	4.4	2.7	33	64
Denmark	48	18.2	5.6	14.3	3.9	79	70
Finland	71	35.2	8.4	16.5	5.4	47	64
France	50	22.5	6.1	10.6	3.4	47	56
Germany	47	14.0	3.4	5.8	1.6	41	47
Greece	—	57.1	24.5	20.2	13.8	35	56
Iceland	80	22.9	10.3	10.6	9.7	46	94
Ireland	41	37.3	15.0	21.8	9.6	58	64
Italy	61	32.6	9.0	12.3	3.1	38	34
Japan	—	30.2	7.2	13.1	2.5	43	35
Luxembourg	—	16.6	3.3	7.1	2.1	43	64
Netherlands	37	9.8	4.6	8.9	4.2	91	91
New Zealand	—	14.6	10.6	8.5	8.6	58	81
Norway	50	21.6	6.5	9.0	2.9	42	45
Portugal	65	43.9	17.8	23.5	6.2	54	35
Spain	70	38.7	11.8	22.0	4.5	57	38
Sweden	42	15.7	3.3	4.8	2.6	31	79
Switzerland	61	14.5	5.6	—	2.5	—	45
Turkey	—	75.9	47.8	38.0	15.4	50	32
United Kingdom	15	4.7	2.1	3.4	1.3	72	62
United States	—	8.5	2.8	3.9	2.0	46	71
Total OECD	—	21.6	7.5	7.2	2.7	53	59

SOURCES: OECD, *Historical Statistics* (1993b); *National Accounts* (1993c); Mitchell, *European Historical Statistics, 1750-1975*, table B1 (1980).

[a] When the figure for 1990 is not available, the latest available figure is recorded.

This is the bright side of Baumol's law: it still takes four to play a string quartet and always will, but it takes fewer and fewer farmers to feed the rest of us.[1] Just as the interplay between highly elastic demand and stagnant productivity in the performing arts causes a persistent increase in production costs relative to those of other industries where productivity rises over time (Throsby, 1994), so the interaction of rapid technological progress and inelastic demand makes agriculture steadily more expensive to maintain. Increasing costs in the arts and decreasing costs in agriculture have similar effects as well as causes: they tend to depress the incomes of artists and farmers and to generate steadily increasing demands for subsidies. It is thus not technological progress as such that depresses farm incomes over time, but rather the interaction of technological progress with the biological inelasticity of the demand for food.

In 1870-71, at the time of the Franco-German war, the labor of every second Frenchman and German was required to feed the French and German populations. Today, with modern farming techniques, roughly the same job—indeed, a much better job—is done by one-tenth to one-twentieth the number of farmers. What happened to the others? They were released to work in other industries and thus to contribute to the buildup of strong, diversified, modern economies based on industry, trade, and services.

Figure 1 highlights the relation between the decline of agriculture and economic growth in the world. The vertical axis shows the share of agriculture in GDP in 105 low-, middle-, and high-income economies; the horizontal axis shows their real GDP per capita. With a correlation of −0.86, the general pattern is clear: poor countries are overwhelmingly agricultural, whereas rich countries derive their steadily increasing income and wealth primarily from industry, and especially from trade and services. These sectors have grown to account for almost two-thirds of GDP in the industrial countries, compared with about one-half of GDP on average in middle-income developing countries, about two-fifths on average in low-income developing countries, and even less than that

[1] According to Baumol's law, the performing arts and other labor-intensive activities, such as education and health care, inevitably become more expensive over time relative to most other economic activities. This is because labor productivity in the arts and these other fields is generally stagnant, whereas productivity rises and costs of production fall over time in other activities. This is an important reason for the persistent and escalating financial difficulties of theaters and other cultural institutions and for steadily heavier tax and public-debt burdens in countries where schools and hospitals are operated mostly by the government (Baumol and Bowen, 1966).

FIGURE 1

AGRICULTURE AND PER CAPITA OUTPUT IN 105 ECONOMIES, 1991

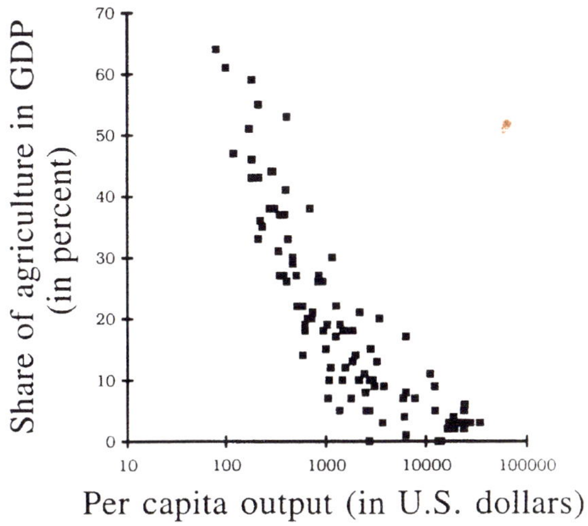

SOURCES: World Bank, *World Development Report*, appendix tables 1 and 3 (1993); OECD, *National Accounts* (1993c).

in most of the erstwhile planned economies of Central and Eastern Europe (World Bank, 1993).

The Cultural Case for Agricultural Protection

The gradual but massive transfer of labor from farms in Europe and elsewhere has created, or threatened to create, severe economic and social problems, especially for uprooted farmers and their families. This is the essence of the farm problem and a prime justification for ambitious agricultural policies intended to resist the trend toward fewer, more efficient farms and to alleviate the burden of relocation from farm to city. It is not the sole source of the problem, however. The biological inelasticity of the demand for food makes farm prices and incomes uncommonly sensitive to supply shocks, and a technological innovation or a bumper crop can thus reduce farm prices and incomes drastically. In a world with imperfect private insurance markets, price and income stabilization is, therefore, another important objective of agricultural policies. If farmers could insure themselves in private markets against adverse supply shocks, the case for government stabilization programs would be weaker. In addition, farm protection is often regarded as an instrument of regional policy; agriculture is shielded from market forces to secure a desired distribution of the population across regions and to protect certain rural areas from depopulation.

Specifically, according to the Treaty of Rome, the major goals of the CAP of the European Union (EU) are to:

(1) increase agricultural productivity;
(2) insure a fair standard of living for the farm community;
(3) stabilize farm-product markets;
(4) provide food security; and
(5) secure supplies to consumers at reasonable prices.

These objectives are not mutually consistent in all respects. In particular, the aim of raising farm incomes may, and often does, conflict with the goals of securing low prices for consumers and of increasing agricultural productivity—the latter because the CAP, by protecting small and often inefficient farms, has stood in the way of exploiting scale economies in agriculture.

Why do governments pay particular attention to the natural and inevitable trend toward fewer, more efficient farms? Do they resist with similar fervor the replacement of old coal mines by cleaner, more efficient sources of energy? In fact, they do. According to Radetzki (1994), coal production in France, Germany, Spain, and the United Kingdom is subsidized directly and indirectly at a cost of almost $60,000 per job. Unlike coal mining, however, agriculture has a special place in the hearts and minds of Europeans and many others—a place, indeed, that lies beyond the purview of pure economics. Farmers—some farmers, at least—are viewed as artists. They contribute to society and culture by bringing us *brie* and *gorgonzola*, by keeping the countryside populated, green, and clean, and by preserving our common cultural heritage and our treasured links to the land. They can be considered to generate external benefits that justify public financial support on similar grounds as the arts. Parisians and most other city dwellers are willing to pay for the preservation of agriculture because they think it enriches their lives, and especially if they feel that farming is in some way an endangered occupation. Unlike most industrial plants, farms cannot be left entirely to the vagaries of the market because external benefits are involved. Without support, there would simply be too few farmers. Agriculture, like art, is something of a public good. This perception is an important part of the reason why every industrial country (with the recent exception of New Zealand) supports its farmers in some measure. In many developing countries, by contrast, agriculture remains the main occupation and, rather than receiving support, is a major source of direct and indirect tax revenue to the governments (World Bank, 1986). Indeed, the taxation of agriculture in developing countries, where poor farmers are commonly taxed, directly and indirectly, by about 30 percent, shows that farm subsidization is by no means the natural order of things (Schiff and Valdés, 1992). It can, however, be explained by the cultural argument, which produces broad-based consent to support for agriculture.

Because the cultural argument for farm support is clearly normative, it is impossible to refute in its general form—and it appears in many guises. Some OECD countries have counted among the explicit objectives of their agricultural policies the maintenance of healthy rural communities, the promotion of regional development, the preservation and encouragement of family farming, the protection of the environment, and even national security. These are commendable objectives, but empirical evidence suggests that the CAP is not effective, efficient, or equitable in reaching them. The CAP has neither provided adequate incomes to small-scale farmers nor preserved and encouraged family farming. Instead, it has generated windfall gains for more efficient, large-scale farmers, especially by pushing up rents and land prices (Rosenblatt et al., 1988; Martin et al., 1989/90). In addition, capital subsidies under the CAP have encouraged excessive use of chemical fertilizers that appear to have polluted rather than preserved the environment (Winters, 1989/90; Anderson, 1992a). This suggests that less, not more, agriculture in Europe would be good for the countryside and that the environmental part of the cultural argument for farm support can begin to apply only after agriculture has contracted further. The national-security argument for agricultural protection, often heard in Russia and Japan, is not convincing either. Not even during World War II were entire countries cut off from foreign food supplies.

The CAP has also led to extensive and wasteful overproduction of farm goods, drawing resources from industry, trade, and services and calling for enormous public expenditure on agriculture at the expense of other needs. It has, in addition, distorted incentives by raising food prices in Europe, thus imparting a stagflationary bias to the European economy and worsening the terms of trade of many food-exporting countries in the rest of the world, especially the developing countries. These problems have been compounded by imperfect competition in agricultural markets in individual countries (a case in point is the Dutch milk monopoly, whereby one company in the Netherlands has a virtual monopoly in the milk market). The result of all this has been substantial waste in terms of welfare lost and nonagricultural output foregone.

Although there may be a cultural argument for maintaining farm protection at present levels, direct and indirect public outlays on agriculture need to be compared fairly and squarely with other cultural outlays and with the external benefits they generate. Such comparisons are difficult to make, but they are likely to indicate a substantial overcommitment to agriculture. This reflects the fact that farmers and landowners are a vocal and well-organized interest group in Europe and elsewhere in the industrial countries, where their political influence is often disproportionate to their numbers (Bohlin, Meyersson, and Ståhl, 1984; Gardner, 1992). In some countries, farm regions are grossly overrepresented in national legislative bodies (Iceland, Japan, and Norway are cases in point), and individuals with close ties to agricultural interests are even chosen to head ministries of agriculture, which then tend to guard special interests against the public interest, rather than the other way around. Russia, before and after the revolution of 1991, is an extreme example of this tendency and its macroeconomic consequences.

Why do agricultural special interests tend to prevail over the public interest? It is true that each farmer and landowner stands to gain much more from protection than each consumer and taxpayer stands to lose (Sharker, Meilke, and Hoy, 1993; Anderson, 1994), but this is a general argument that applies to other sectors as well. A better explanation may derive from the fact that agriculture accounts for less than 3 percent of national income on average in the industrial countries. Its relative unimportance and its continuing decline may have created a general impression that agricultural protection cannot be all that costly. This impression may have been supported by poor information; data collection and monitoring of agricultural policies by national authorities and international organizations were lax and inadequate at least until the late 1980s. If poor information is a factor in farm protection, it is especially urgent to assess accurately the full cost of support and to make the general public and policymakers aware of the cost.

The Cost of Agricultural Protection

The main instrument of the CAP is price support. It is maintained by intervention purchases, as well as variable import levies, export refunds (that is, subsidies), deficiency payments, and production quotas. This strategy has two major implications in Europe: it raises food prices for consumers, and it imposes higher taxes on taxpayers. Consumers are thus deprived of access to less expensive imported agricultural products, and taxpayers must accept reduced purchasing power in order to finance the fiscal needs of the CAP. Until the early 1980s, it was this direct fiscal cost of farm protection that attracted most attention in empirical studies. More recently, however, attention has also been drawn to the even more important indirect cost of protection through the price support that has inflated food prices in Europe.

This is not all, however. Agricultural protection in Europe and elsewhere imposes two other types of potentially major costs: (1) costs to industry, trade, and services, which are taxed implicitly by the favorable treatment of agriculture and (2) costs to the rest of the world, especially the developing countries and, more recently, the countries of Central and Eastern Europe, the agricultural products of which have been denied access to the European market. To assess the full cost of farm protection, all these factors need to be taken into account.

How large, then, is the current cost of agricultural protection in Europe and elsewhere among the OECD countries?

In 1992, the total cost imposed on consumers and taxpayers in the OECD amounted to more than $350 billion (Table 2). This amount is larger than the combined GDPs of Australia and New Zealand and only slightly smaller than the combined GDPs of Austria and Switzerland. Direct transfers from taxpayers have tended to be the favored method of farm protection in Australia, Canada, and the United States. Indirect transfers from consumers are relatively larger in Europe, and even larger in Japan, where the domestic price of rice, the main staple food, has been five to seven times higher than the world market price in recent years.

The transfer-cost figures shown in Table 2 are *gross*. To estimate the *net* cost of agricultural protection in classic textbook fashion, that is, the deadweight or welfare loss, one would need to subtract the benefits received by farmers and landowners from the gross costs to consumers and taxpayers. As Johnson (1991, chap. 3) suggests, however, the net cost is not an obviously better measure of the burden than the gross cost. To see this, consider a scheme in which the poor pay a lump-sum tax of 100 in order to subsidize the rich by the same amount. The textbook measure of the net welfare cost is zero, but the true burden is probably closer to the gross cost of 100, because the poor are hurt much more by the tax than the rich are benefited by the subsidy. Now consider a scheme in which consumers and taxpayers are forced to pay 100 to subsidize the income of farmers by 50 and also to incur a dead-

TABLE 2

TOTAL TRANSFERS ASSOCIATED WITH AGRICULTURAL POLICIES IN THE OECD COUNTRIES, 1992
(*in billions of U.S. dollars*)

Country or Area	Transfers from Taxpayers	Transfers from Consumers	Budget Revenues	Total Transfers[a]
Australia	1.1	0.4	0.0	1.6
Austria	1.3	3.0	0.1	4.2
Canada	5.4	3.7	0.0	9.1
EU	67.0	89.7	0.8	155.9
Finland	1.9	2.8	0.1	4.5
Japan	18.0	68.8	12.8	74.0
New Zealand	0.0	0.0	0.0	0.1
Norway	2.2	2.1	0.1	4.1
Sweden	0.6	2.9	0.3	3.2
Switzerland	2.6	3.9	0.7	5.8
United States	63.4	28.6	0.9	91.1
Total OECD	163.6	205.9	15.8	353.7

SOURCE: OECD, *Agricultural Policies, Markets and Trade, Monitoring and Outlook*, table II.15 (1993a).

NOTE: Detail is rounded and may not add to totals. For a description of the methods by which these estimates were generated, including assumptions about demand and supply elasticities and wage rigidities, see OECD, *National Policies* (1987) and *OECD Economic Studies*, 13 (1989/90).

[a]Total transfers equal transfers from taxpayers and consumers *minus* budget revenues.

weight loss of 50 because they must also pay the salaries of agriculture ministry officials, the cost of storing food surpluses, and so on. Clearly, the true cost in this case is not zero, because bureaucrats, storage owners, and other nonfarmers at the receiving end would presumably find other worthy and equally remunerative things to do if the scheme were dismantled. But if this analysis applies to the bureaucrats and to other middlemen, why should it not also apply to the extra income enjoyed by the farmers and landowners? They, too, might find other and equally remunerative activities.

A comparable preference for measuring burdens by gross rather than net cost explains in part why white-collar crime is illegal. Because the main purpose of such crime is to redistribute wealth without violence, the net cost involved is probably near zero; understandably, however, the gross cost matters more to most people in this case.

It is therefore far from obvious that the benefits that farmers and landowners receive from agricultural protection should be subtracted from the costs imposed on consumers and taxpayers to arrive at the true burden of farm protection, not least in view of the fundamentally regressive nature of the transfers. Not only do inflated food prices fall most heavily on poor families, but in the long run, the benefits of farm support accrue primarily to landowners, and then mostly to those who own the largest estates (Winters, 1987; Martin et al., 1989/90). This is not surprising. Price support raises rents because land is essentially fixed in supply, but it cannot raise the return to farm labor, because the potential entry of workers into agriculture from other sectors is unrestricted, and price support cannot be used to prevent the inevitable exit of labor from agriculture in the long run. According to Johnson (1991), a sixth or at most a fifth of all farmers in the industrial countries are responsible for two-thirds to three-fourths of all farm sales and receive support commensurately. In view of all this, both gross and net estimates of the cost of farm protection are presented below.

The OECD estimates of gross cost shown in Table 2 are based on elaborate computations of Producer Subsidy Equivalents (PSEs), defined as the decrease in the gross income of producers that would occur if farm protection were discontinued, and Consumer Subsidy Equivalents (CSEs), defined as the increase in consumer expenditures (net of transfers) that would occur if the protection were discontinued. In other words:

PSE equals the quantity produced *times* the difference between the domestic producer price and the world market price *plus* net transfers to agriculture, (1)

CSE equals the subsidies to consumers *minus* the quantity consumed *times* the difference between the domestic consumer price and the world market price. (2)

The PSE and CSE measure transfers to agriculture from domestic consumers and taxpayers resulting from a given set of agricultural policies, but they do not provide a complete picture of all (that is, total) transfers. They cover only a part of the total value of agricultural production (ranging from 54 percent in Japan to 94 percent in Finland), and they exclude transfers due to agricultural and certain food and environmental policies that do not necessarily benefit agriculture alone. The estimates of total transfers shown in Table 2 are defined as the sum of all transfers from taxpayers *plus* all transfers from consumers *minus* estimated budget receipts from tariffs on agricultural imports. Transfers from taxpayers include various budgetary outlays that are excluded from the PSE and CSE calculations, but like the PSE, they exclude outlays on general government administration and social security. Thus, the OECD's assessment of total transfers shown in Table 2 draws upon and extends the estimates of PSEs and CSEs as defined above, essentially by incorporating additional budgetary payments and revenues (OECD, 1993a).

When measured as proportions of GDP, the total gross cost of agricultural support ranged from virtually nil in New Zealand, where transfers to agriculture have been dismantled in recent years as part of the country's radical and ultimately successful economic transformation, to more than 4 percent in Finland (Table 3). Four members of the European Free Trade Association (EFTA) included in Tables 2 and 3 (Austria, Finland, Norway, and Switzerland) spend considerably more on their agriculture relative to GDP than does the European Union (Sweden is an exception). The EFTA countries as a group spend on average about 3 percent of their GDP on agriculture compared with about 2 percent of GDP in the EU.[2]

Table 3 shows that the cost of farm protection is spread quite unevenly across countries. Averages, such as the 2 percent figure for the EU, may thus conceal substantial differences among individual countries. In fact, some countries may gain from farm protection; among EU members, for example, Denmark, France, Ireland, and the Netherlands, are major food exporters. If they gain from farm protection, the losses incurred by other countries included in the corresponding average must be that much larger. A wide range of gains and losses across countries and commodities does not, therefore, necessarily weaken the case against protection. On the contrary, it may strengthen it.

Total per capita agricultural transfers are highest in Norway, where, at $970 per person, they exceed the average for the EU and the OECD countries by more than 100 percent. Total agricultural transfers per full-time farmer equivalent (FFE, defined as 2,200 hours of work in agriculture per year) are highest in Norway and Sweden, where total transfers amount to almost $40,000 per FFE, compared with $17,700 in the EU. Each full-time farmer thus costs consumers and taxpayers more than the median labor income of about $12,000 in the EU, and far more than that in some countries.

[2] On January 1, 1995, Austria, Finland, and Sweden joined the EU.

TABLE 3

TOTAL AGRICULTURAL TRANSFERS IN THE OECD COUNTRIES, 1992

Country or Area	Percent Share of GDP	Dollars per Capita	Dollars per Full-Time Farmer	Dollars per Hectare of Farmland
Australia	0.5	89	4,200	3
Austria	2.3	530	16,400	1,210
Canada	1.6	330	20,400	123
EU	2.0	450	17,700	1,120
Finland	4.1	910	31,300	1,780
Japan	2.0	600	24,000	14,120
New Zealand	0.1	15	400	4
Norway	3.7	970	39,600	4,240
Sweden	1.3	370	38,600	950
Switzerland	2.4	840	29,300	2,850
United States	1.5	360	36,100	210
Total OECD	2.1	440	21,900	310

SOURCE: OECD, *Agricultural Policies, Markets and Trade, Monitoring and Outlook*, tables II.16-II.19 (1993a).

It is striking that agricultural protection per FFE is more than twice as large in the United States as in the EU. Farm support in the United States has not declined in tandem with agricultural employment, which is lower relative to total employment in the United States than in Europe, except in Belgium and the United Kingdom (Table 1, panel 1). Total agricultural transfers per hectare of farmland, however, are highest by far in Japan ($14,000), followed by Norway and Switzerland.

In sum, then, the costs to consumers and taxpayers of protecting agriculture are substantial in all the OECD countries except Australia and New Zealand. In Norway, the gross cost of farm protection exceeds the contribution of agriculture to GDP by almost 1 percent of GDP (compare Table 3 and Table 1, panel 2). Hence, the value added in Norwegian agriculture is negative. In Japan and the United States, the value added in agriculture amounts to about 0.5 percent of GDP.

What happens when the benefits that accrue to farmers are subtracted from the gross-cost figures reviewed above? The mean estimate of the deadweight loss incurred by redistributing incomes from consumers and taxpayers to farmers and landowners is about 1 percent of the EU's GDP (Winters, 1987; Demekas et al., 1988; Rosenblatt et al., 1988). This loss estimate implies a transfer ratio of about 2 (the transfers from consumers and taxpayers are twice as large as the benefits received by farmers and landowners). This is by no means the end of the story, however. One must still consider the discrimination involved against industry, trade, and services and the wasteful rent-seeking, lobbying, investment distortions and even fraud, as well as the hardships imposed on innocent third parties in the rest of the world.

Other evidence. Table 4 gives an overview of several empirical studies of the cost of farm protection in Europe. The numbers in the table are net of the benefits received by farmers. The corresponding gross figures are considerably higher. For example, the net cost of the CAP reported by the Australian Bureau of Agricultural Economics, equivalent to 0.3 percent of GDP, conceals substantial consumer and taxpayer losses, equivalent to 1.2 percent and 1.0 percent of GDP.

The potential output gains from agricultural liberalization implied by the table involve employment gains as well. For example, the 3.3 percent output gain to West Germany reported by Dicke et al. (1988) is consistent with a decrease in unemployment by 4 percent. Similarly, using a general-equilibrium model, Dicke et al. (1988) report a gain of two to four million jobs in Europe as a whole as a result of agricultural liberalization, depending on the degree of real-wage flexibility. The deflationary impact of the CAP is primarily the consequence of domestic agricultural prices being far above world market prices. The price differential in the EU was about 50 percent on average from 1970 to 1985 (Rosenblatt et al., 1988), with the nominal rate of protection ranging from 11 percent for beef to 80 percent for sugar. Tyers and Anderson (1986b) report similar figures. By their calculations, producer-to-border price ratios were 1.6 and 2.2 on average in 1980-82 and 1988 in the EU, compared with 1.9 and 3.2 in the EFTA countries, 2.4 and 3.8 in Japan, and 1.2 and 1.5 in the United States. By 1988 to 1991, the nominal rate of protection had reached 84 percent in the EU, compared with 176 percent in the EFTA countries, 190 percent in Japan, and 33 percent in the United States (OECD, 1992). The corresponding figures for Australia, Canada, and New Zealand from 1988 to 1991 were 13 percent, 48 percent, and 6 percent (Anderson, 1994).

In the partial-equilibrium studies reviewed in Table 4, the figures are intended to reflect deadweight losses in farm-product markets (as measured by Harberger triangles), without regard to the implications of agricultural support for other parts of the economy. In the general-equilibrium studies, by contrast, including those in Stoeckel, Vincent, and Cuthbertson (1989), an attempt has been made to incorporate the long-run economywide ramifications of agricultural protection without, however, taking account of the costs imposed on other countries. The

TABLE 4

THE COST OF AGRICULTURAL SUPPORT IN THE EU IN THE 1980S
(net of benefits to farmers)

Study	Type of Model[a]	Cost of CAP in Percent of GDP	Transfer Ratio[b]
Morris (1980)	PE	0.5	1.4
Thomson and Harvey (1981)	PE	—	1.8
Buckwell et al. (1982)	PE	0.6	1.5
Bureau of Agricultural Economics (1985)	PE	0.5	1.2
Bureau of Agricultural Economics (1985)	PE	0.3	1.2
Burniaux and Waelbroeck (1985)	GE	2.7	—
Spencer (1985)	PE	0.9	—
Tyers (1985)	PE	1.1	3.2
Tyers and Anderson (1986a)	PE	1.3	1.9
OECD (1987)	PE	1.2[c]	
Tyers and Anderson (1987)	PE	0.3	1.2
Dicke et al. (1988)	GE	3.3	—
Rosenblatt et al. (1988)	GE	3.5	—
Stoeckel and Breckling (1989)	GE	1.5	—
Martin et al. (1989/90)	GE	1.4	—
Average		1.4	1.7

[a]PE = partial equilibrium. GE = general equilibrium.

[b]The transfer ratio is defined as the cost in ecu of transferring 1 ecu from consumers and taxpayers to farmers. In other words, the transfer ratio measures the total transfers from consumers and taxpayers as a proportion of the transfers received by farmers.

[c]This figure is obtained by taking the gross estimate reported, 2.8 percent, of the costs of transfers from consumers and taxpayers and converting it to a net figure by subtracting the transfers to farmers, using the average transfer ratio of 1.7 shown in the bottom right corner of the table.

general-equilibrium studies yield higher cost estimates than the partial-equilibrium studies (Buckwell and Medland, 1991). On average, they are about three times as high as those obtained from partial-equilibrium studies, or 2.2 percent versus 0.7 percent of GDP in the two types of models reviewed in the table. This is partly because the long-run general-equilibrium studies typically assume larger price elasticities of agricultural supply than the more short-run partial-equilibrium studies (see, for example, Miller and Spencer, 1977, and Johnson, 1991, chap. 6). There are other reasons as well; the basic differences between partial-equilibrium and general-equilibrium analysis are discussed below.

Broadly similar results have been reported in several other studies and for other countries. Bale and Lutz (1981) found, for example, that the cost to consumers of agricultural policy in the United Kingdom, France, Germany, and Japan ranged from 0.5 percent to 1.4 percent of their GNP in 1976. Otsuka and Hayami concluded that the net cost of Japanese rice policy alone from 1965 to 1980 amounted to between 0.3 percent and 0.7 percent of Japan's GDP. In Japan and Korea, agricultural liberalization would raise real wages by 3 percent and 6 percent, respectively, according to Vincent (1989a, 1989b), while land prices would fall by 70 percent and 45 percent. Martin et al. (1989/90), in some of their general-equilibrium computations, found that GDP in the EU would rise by between 3 percent and 6 percent following multilateral liberalization of agricultural support in the OECD countries, and that agricultural output would fall by about 18 percent. They report, moreover, that the total cost of farm support per job saved in agriculture and food processing ranges from $13,000 in Japan and $20,000 in the EU and the United States to almost $100,000 in Canada (at 1988 prices and exchange rates). Many more examples could be given.

The Uruguay Round of the GATT. In the Uruguay Round, agricultural protection was, for the first time, brought seriously under GATT discipline. The cost of agricultural protection is scheduled to be reduced significantly over the next few years both by reducing direct transfers to agriculture and by replacing nontariff trade barriers by more efficient and transparent tariffs that will then be reduced by 36 percent over a period of six years ending in 2001. That way, with high tariff rates visible for everyone to see, the farm lobby will find it more difficult than before to dispute empirical estimates of the total cost of agricultural protection. This is an important accomplishment.

Even so, at the end of this six-year adjustment period, the costs to consumers and taxpayers of protecting agriculture will remain high. Moreover, as Johnson (1991) points out, a constant degree of protection is not enough to maintain farm incomes at a given level. This is because a price increase raises farm incomes once and for all. Therefore, a continuous increase in agricultural support is needed to enable farm incomes to keep pace with steadily increasing real incomes in the rest of the economy. The persistent tendency for farm support in Europe to increase over time is, therefore, no coincidence. On the contrary, it is a direct consequence of the fact that productivity growth exceeds demand growth by more in agriculture than in other economic activities. The widening discrepancy between farm and nonfarm incomes leads to a continuous flow of labor out of agriculture and fuels demands for steadily increased farm subsidies over time to stem the tide.

These tendencies are borne out by experience. According to the OECD (1992), the nominal rate of agricultural protection in industrial countries rose persistently between 1979-81 and 1988-91: from 58 percent to 84 percent in the EU, from 133 percent to 190 percent in Japan, from 19 percent to 33 percent in the United States, from 32 percent to 48 percent in Canada, and from 41 percent to 73 percent in the OECD as a whole. Looking further back, Gulbrandsen and Lindbeck (1973) estimate that the average nominal rate of agricultural protection in Western Europe increased from less than 30 percent in the 1930s to more than 60 percent in the late 1960s. In Japan, rice imports were free before 1904, but after a tariff was imposed that year, the rate of rice protection rose to more than 60 percent by the late 1930s and to more than 700 percent by the late 1980s (Anderson, 1994; Tyers and Anderson, 1986b). The general intensification of agricultural protection has coincided with a gradual liberalization of trade in industrial goods.

In this connection, it is interesting that many economists and politicians who advocate shock therapy as the best way of securing effective economic liberalization in Central and Eastern Europe seem nevertheless to favor a gradual approach to farm-trade liberalization at home, even though several but perhaps not all of the standard arguments against gradualism would seem to apply to trade reform in general. In particular, many have argued forcefully that delayed adjustment in the former socialist economies only prolongs the pain and plays into the hands of special-interest groups, which gain time and opportunity to organize opposition and even sabotage reforms. The macroeconomic consequences of the chosen gradual approach to farm-policy reform and to agricultural-trade liberalization need to be pondered in this light.

2 THE MACROECONOMIC IMPLICATIONS OF AGRICULTURAL PROTECTION

The cost of agricultural protection was generally considered light, or at least not a major political concern, as long as the European economies enjoyed full employment and healthy economic growth in the decades following World War II. In times of hardship, high and increasing unemployment, and sluggish growth, however, all available means of increasing macroeconomic efficiency and restoring full employment and rapid growth should be considered. The scope for farm-policy reform must, therefore, be contemplated along with other options. As long as European consumers and taxpayers continue to pay, on average, the equivalent of about 2 percent or more of Europe's GDP every year for agricultural protection, agriculture will be a major macroeconomic concern.

The case against agricultural protection is closely related to the case against protectionism in general. It relates not only to the welfare losses and leakages involved in the redistribution of income from consumers and taxpayers to farmers and landowners, but also to the need to uproot the inefficiency involved in impeding agricultural markets and trade and foregoing income and expenditure opportunities at home and abroad. It is therefore necessary to go beyond the partial-equilibrium measures of the cost of farm protection reviewed above (Tables 2 and 3).

Gains from Trade

Imagine two sectors, agriculture and industry, where productive resources are fully but inefficiently employed, initially because the price of agricultural goods relative to industrial goods is higher at home than in world markets. Agricultural produce is overpriced—by about 80 percent on average in Europe, according to the OECD (1992)—and more resources are therefore devoted to farm production than would be the case under free trade at world market prices. When all restrictions on farm trade are lifted, trade takes place at undistorted world market prices. Agricultural output contracts without protection, at least initially, but industrial production expands, and total output in the economy increases as intended (Figure 2). There is thus scope for those who gain from the change to compensate those who lose. In view

FIGURE 2

OUTPUT GAIN FROM AGRICULTURAL-TRADE LIBERALIZATION

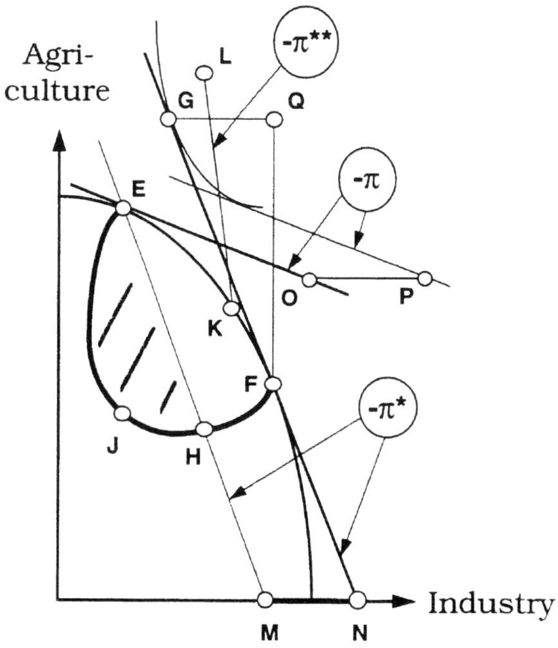

of the regressive nature of current farm protection in Europe, however, it is not clear that substantial compensation would in fact be paid.

In Figure 2, the initial full-employment equilibrium position is described by point *E*, where the domestic relative-price line (with a slope of $-\pi$) is tangential to the production-possibility frontier. At *E*, domestic production equals domestic consumption, and no trade takes place, because of a prohibitive tariff or its equivalent by assumption. The steeper line (with a slope of $-\pi^*$) describes the ratio of the prices of the two goods in world markets. The intersection of this line through *E* and the horizontal axis gives total output (GDP) measured in industrial goods, using world prices.

Suppose now that all restrictions on farm trade are lifted. Trade begins at undistorted world market prices. Agricultural output contracts. The economy moves downward from *E* to a point such as *J*, inside the production-possibility frontier. Unemployment emerges. If the contraction of agricultural production spreads to industry, that is, if the decline in purchasing power in agriculture reduces the demand for industrial goods as well, industrial production first falls and then rises again on the way from *E* to *J*. Aggregate output is lower at *J* than at *E*. Sooner or later, however, the increase in the relative price of industrial goods will begin to be exploited by profit-seeking entrepreneurs. As resources are transferred from agriculture and idleness to industry, the economy begins to move to the right from the interior point *J* toward point *F* on the production-possibility frontier.

One possible adjustment path is described by the locus *EJHF*. Along the segment *EJ*, output is lower than it was initially in both agriculture and industry. At *J*, industrial output is restored to its original level, but national output is still lower than it was initially. At *H*, national output has returned to its initial level, but full employment is not restored until the new equilibrium point *F* is reached. Gradual adjustment trajectories of this type involving unemployment of labor and other factors of production reflect optimal producer behavior if the adjustment process itself is costly (for example, the cost of training workers moving from agriculture to industry).

When point *F* on the production-possibility frontier is reached, aggregate output measured in industrial goods has increased by an amount indicated by the thick segment *MN* of the horizontal axis in the figure. Domestic production of agricultural and industrial goods in the new equilibrium is described by point *F* in the figure, and domestic consumption, by point *G*. The concave shape of the production-possibility frontier reflecting the law of diminishing returns insures that agriculture does not disappear. Industrial goods are now exported in exchange for agricultural imports from the rest of the world. The trade triangle is shown by *GQF*. At world market prices, exports *GQ* are equal to imports *FQ*. The current account is in equilibrium.

The welfare cost of the status quo is another matter. This cost is measured by the additional resources that would be required at domestic prices without trade to lift the economy to the same level of social welfare as could be achieved by structural adjustment through free trade. The welfare cost in terms of industrial production measured at domestic prices is indicated by the horizontal distance *OP* between the domestic relative-price line (with a slope of $-\pi$) tangential to the production-possibility frontier at point *E* and the parallel price line tangential to the upper social-indifference curve that goes through point *G*. Generally, this hypothetical welfare cost of the status quo, *OP*, is different from the output gain from structural adjustment, *MN*, denoted by the thick segment of the horizontal axis.

Because of its weight in world markets and its ability to affect world prices, the European Union might be able to gain from less than full liberalization of farm trade. Partial liberalization, as, for example, from *E* to *K* in Figure 2 could result in more favorable terms of trade for Europe, as reflected by the line segment (with a slope of $-\pi^{**}$) connecting the production point *K* and the corresponding consumption point *L*. Welfare at *L* under the optimum tariff would then exceed welfare at *G* under free trade.

The total output gain described thus far reflects only the intersectoral reallocation of resources, not increased efficiency in the use of those resources within each sector over time. As emphasized by Koester (1991), farm output may actually increase following liberalization, as farmers are encouraged to adopt new technologies and as efficient farmers expand their operations to fill the void left by less efficient farmers who leave the land. This explains why total farm output in New Zealand has grown by 2 to 4 percent a year since farm protection was discontinued in 1984. The production of some commodities, such as wine, fruits, and nuts, has grown by leaps and bounds following the liberalization (see Box 1).

The efficiency improvement in the use of resources in each sector is shown by the outward shift of the production-possibility frontier from *AB* to *AC* in Figure 3, and by the change of the production pattern from *F* to *G*, where farm output is higher than it was initially at *E*. Of the total increase in output, indicated by the thick line segment *MQ* on the horizontal axis in the figure, *MN* stems from the liberalization (as in Figure 2), and *NQ* stems from the resulting rise in productivity. In Leibenstein's (1966) terminology, *MN* reflects increased allocative efficiency and *NQ* reflects increased X-efficiency.

The total output gain (measured at world prices) from free farm trade depends on three features: (1) the magnitude of the initial trade distortion, (2) the response of technology to trade, as reflected by the outward shift of the production-possibility frontier in Figure 3, and (3) the flexibility of production, as reflected by the curvature of the production-possibility frontier shown in Figure 2. As shown in Appendix A, the expansion of total output measured at world prices is approximately proportional to the square of the original trade distortion:

$$\text{Expansion} = mc^2 , \tag{3}$$

where m is a multiplicative factor that reflects the shape and shift of the production-possibility frontier and c is a measure of the constant initial

BOX 1

FARMING WITHOUT SUBSIDIES: THE CASE OF NEW ZEALAND

In 1950, New Zealand was the third-richest country in the world measured in national per capita income. The country had no unemployment, no inflation to speak of, and almost no foreign debt. Gradually, its economy declined—to eleventh place in the rich-country club in 1960, to fifteenth place in 1970, to twentieth place in 1980, and to twenty-third place in 1987 (Crocombe, Enright, and Porter, 1991). Living standards worsened. Unemployment, inflation, and especially external debt, rose to unprecedented levels.

This decline can be traced in part to reduced access of New Zealand's agricultural products to the U.K. market after the United Kingdom entered the European Economic Community in 1973, and partly also to extensive protectionism at home. The nominal rate of pastoral agricultural protection in New Zealand, for example, reached a peak of 123 percent in 1982-83, the highest rate in the OECD.

The withdrawal of farm subsidies in 1984 involved significant adjustment costs. About 800 farms—one in a hundred—failed. Farmers leaving the land were given "exit grants" equivalent to about two-thirds of their annual income. Even with this decrease, however, the number of full-time farm workers had recovered by 1991 to the pre-1984 level. Farm commodity prices fell by 15 to 65 percent in real terms (Koester, 1991), real incomes on sheep and beef farms decreased by 40 percent, and real farmland values dropped comparably, but real incomes on dairy farms did not decline. "On balance," the OECD (1991, p. 63) reported, "agricultural reform has resulted in a stronger, more diversified and resilient agricultural sector." Efficiency has improved through larger farms, new technology, and mechanization. New products and new markets have been developed. Land use and input use per acre have decreased in favor of more labor-intensive production. The main losers have been landowners and banks whose assets had to be devalued to prevent the insolvency of many farms (Koester, 1991).

trade distortion shown by the angle between the domestic and world market price lines, as described in Figures 2 and 3. This equation shows the output gain in general equilibrium by taking into full account the expansion of industry resulting from the liberalization of farm trade and by including the potential efficiency gains that result from the liberalization. The same equation is obtained when total output is measured in terms of a consumer price index defined as a weighted average of agricultural and industrial prices, rather than in units of industrial output measured at world prices.

This simple formula for output gain is a variation on a well-known theme in welfare economics: the welfare gain from removing a single

FIGURE 3

OUTPUT GAIN FROM AGRICULTURAL-TRADE LIBERALIZATION AND TECHNOLOGICAL PROGRESS

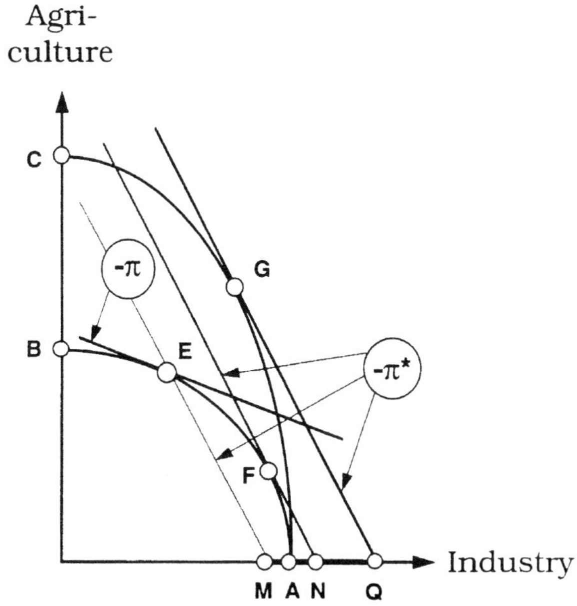

distortion (a tax or a tariff, for example) is proportional to the square of the initial distortion (Harberger, 1964).

Partial versus General Equilibrium

Equation (3) can now be used to approximate the potential output gains from farm-trade liberalization. As shown in Appendix A, the parameter m in equation (3) is a multiple of several factors: I/Y, which is the share of industry (that is, manufacturing, communications, trade, and services) in total output after the structural adjustment has been completed; b, which is the elasticity of industrial production with respect to its relative price; and k, which is the response of agricultural productivity change to the trade liberalization.

Specifically, we have

$$m = \frac{1}{2}\left(\frac{I}{Y}\right)b\left(1 + k^2\right) . \tag{4}$$

The distortion parameter c in the equation is defined as 1 *minus* the inverse of 1 *plus* the nominal rate of protection, or tariff equivalent (t):

$$c = 1 - \frac{\pi}{\pi^*} = 1 - \frac{1}{1+t} = \frac{t}{1+t}, \qquad (5)$$

where π and π^* are the relative prices of industrial and agricultural goods at home and abroad. Therefore, if domestic farm prices are kept at 80 percent above world market prices ($t = 0.8$), a seemingly reasonable figure for the EU (OECD, 1992; Anderson, 1994), and if the price of industrial goods is the same at home and abroad, it follows that $\pi/\pi^* = 1/1.8 = 0.56$, so that $c = 0.44$.

Table 5 portrays static output gains under various conditions when protection ranges from 20 to 80 percent (and c goes from 0.17 to 0.44). It is assumed that industry in a broad sense (that is, all sectors except agriculture) accounts for 95 percent of total output, that the elasticity of industrial production with respect to its relative price ranges from 0.05 to 0.2 (which means that the long-run price elasticity of farm production ranges from 1 to 4, a plausible range compared with the various estimates reviewed by Johnson (1991, chap. 6), and that the response of farm productivity to the liberalization is reflected in a value of k at 0.7,[1] so that the withdrawal of 80 percent protection increases productivity (that is, X-efficiency) by about 30 percent (see equation [A15]).

On these assumptions, we obtain the approximate estimates of the static output gains from agricultural liberalization shown in Table 5. If the long-run price elasticity is 0.2 and the nominal rate of protection is 80 percent, the potential output gain amounts to almost 3 percent of GNP (see the starred entry in the bottom right corner of the table). This estimate is net; it reflects both the gains to industry and the losses to agriculture following liberalization. Higher elasticity estimates, greater productivity effects, and more severe price distortions initially yield even larger potential output gains.[2] Without the productivity gains, that is, if $k = 0$, all the entries in the table would be reduced by a third. With stronger productivity gains, so that $k = 1$, for example, all the entries would be increased by a third. Moreover, the net gains shown in the table are smaller than the corresponding gross gains, as before.

The general-equilibrium estimate given above is about three times as large as the mean estimate of the deadweight loss from farm protection

[1] This choice is necessarily arbitrary, because no empirical evidence is available on this parameter.

[2] For comparison, the estimate of the permanent static output gain that is expected to emerge gradually from the market unification of Europe after 1992 is about 4 to 5 percent (Cecchini, 1988).

TABLE 5

STATIC OUTPUT GAINS FROM AGRICULTURAL-TRADE LIBERALIZATION AS A FUNCTION OF AGRICULTURAL PROTECTION AND THE ELASTICITY OF INDUSTRIAL SUPPLY

(in percent)

Initial Distortion[a]	Percent Protection	Price Elasticity of Industrial Production: 0.05	0.1	0.2
0.17	20	0.1	0.2	0.4
0.33	50	0.4	0.8	1.6
0.44	80	0.7	1.4	2.8*

SOURCE: Author's computations based on equation (3).

NOTE: Calculations assume the share of industry in GDP is 0.95 and the response of agricultural productivity to trade liberalization is 0.7; productivity rises by the latter (k) *times* the initial distortion (c), or by 31 percent if $k = 0.7$ and $c = 0.44$.

[a] The initial distortion (c) equals 1 *minus* the inverse of 1 *plus* the nominal rate of protection (t), that is, $c = 1 - 1/(1 + t) = t/(1 + t)$, so that $t = \pi^*/\pi - 1 = c/(1 - c)$.

in partial-equilibrium analysis, according to the surveys of the IMF (Rosenblatt et al., 1988) and Winters (1987). To see this clearly, the partial-equilibrium estimates of deadweight loss can be approximated by Harberger's law, which expresses the deadweight welfare loss from a trade distortion (t) as a multiple (v) of the square of the distortion:

$$\text{Loss} = vt^2 . \tag{6}$$

The loss is expressed as a fraction of total output. The constant v equals one-half of the multiple of the import-demand and export-supply elasticities involved (e_d and e_s) *divided* by their sum *times* the share of agriculture in total output (A/Y). Thus,

$$\text{Loss} = \frac{1}{2}\left(\frac{e_d e_s}{e_d + e_s}\right)\left(\frac{A}{Y}\right) t^2 . \tag{7}$$

Figure 4 illustrates equation (7). The deadweight welfare loss is represented by the triangle *ABC* in the short run, and by the larger triangle *ABD* in the long run, when supply becomes infinitely elastic. The area of the triangle *ABC* equals one-half of its base ($t = AB$) *times* its height ($x = EC$). That is, $ABC = ½tx$. The point E divides the line

FIGURE 4
DEADWEIGHT WELFARE LOSS FROM A TRADE DISTORTION

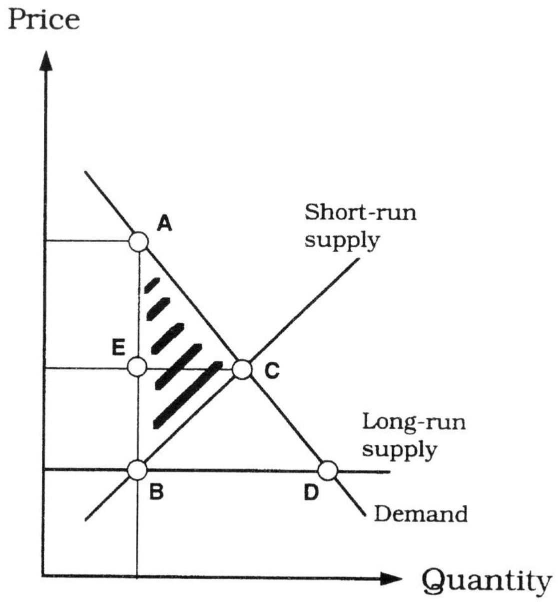

segment AB in two, $AE = at$ and $EB = (1 - a)t$, where $a = AE/AB$. The height x can be written either as $x = atd$ or as $x = (1 - a)ts$, where d and s represent the slopes of the demand and supply schedules. It follows that $a = s/(d + s)$ and $x = [ds/(d + s)]t$, so that $ABC = ½[ds/(d + s)]t^2$. By replacing d and s by the corresponding elasticities, e_d and e_s, and expressing the loss in proportion to total output, we obtain the equation.

If, for example, $e_d = 1$, $e_s = 2$, $A/Y = 0.05$, and $t = 0.8$, the equation implies a loss of about 1 percent of output.[3] This number reflects the loss of consumer surplus in excess of the gain in producer surplus *in agriculture* resulting from inflated farm prices through protection. It does not, however, reflect the other side of the coin, namely, the loss of producer surplus and the gain in consumer surplus *in industry* resulting from depressed industrial prices relative to agriculture (Harberger, 1974). Doubling the price-elasticity estimates from 1 and 2 in the short run to 2 and 4 in the long run also doubles the estimate of the welfare loss, from 1 percent to 2 percent of total output. This,

[3] As the supply elasticity (e_s) approaches infinity, the deadweight welfare loss approaches 1.6 percent of output.

roughly, is how Harberger (1959) concluded that Chile's trade restrictions, which were equivalent to a tariff of 50 percent in the 1950s, involved a welfare loss of at most 2.5 percent of the national income.

The beauty and simplicity of Harberger's formula are probably at least partly to blame for the preponderance of partial-equilibrium studies of the costs of agricultural protection up until the late 1980s (see Table 4). General-equilibrium analysis was less common because it is more complex and has greater computational requirements. When it was used, however, it invariably indicated considerably higher costs of protection than were found by partial-equilibrium methods.

We have seen, however, that the general-equilibrium analysis can be formulated and implemented just as simply as its partial-equilibrium counterpart. The main advantage of the general-equilibrium approach is that it takes into account the response of nonagricultural output to farm-trade liberalization and explicitly assumes a time horizon long enough for all farm inputs to have been gainfully reemployed outside agriculture. It also enables a calculation of X-efficiency gains in the protected sector, because it faces stiffer competition from abroad. The comparison between the simple calculations based on the two methods confirms the substantial downward bias of the short-run partial-equilibrium estimates apparent from Table 4. In this light, it seems reasonable to conclude that the total cost of agricultural protection in Europe and elsewhere is higher than short-run partial-equilibrium analyses have led us to believe.

Trade and Growth

This is not the end of the story. Increased macroeconomic efficiency through free trade increases the output that can be produced from given inputs and is, therefore, tantamount to technological progress. To see this, suppose that output is proportional to capital in a broad sense (as in Romer, 1986, who extended the earlier pioneering work of Domar, 1947, and Harrod, 1948). Then output depends solely on the existing stock of capital and on the efficiency with which it is used in production, as is shown in Appendix B:

$$\text{Output} = \text{efficiency } \textit{times} \text{ capital} . \qquad (8)$$

Put differently, output depends simply on the quantity and quality of capital. By "efficiency" is meant the overall efficiency of resource allocation in the economy. Therefore, all improvements in efficiency count, including those resulting from domestic price reform, foreign-trade liberalization, privatization, education, research and development, and possibly even macroeconomic stabilization.

Moreover, if saving is proportional to output and equals gross investment (net investment *plus* depreciation), then we have

$$\text{Growth} = \text{saving rate } \textit{times} \text{ efficiency } \textit{minus} \text{ depreciation} . \quad (9)$$

More precisely, the rate of economic growth equals the multiple of the saving rate and the efficiency of capital use *minus* the depreciation rate.

By implication, all improvements in efficiency, including farm-trade liberalization, result not only in a higher level of output (equation [3]), but also, through enhanced efficiency in the use of capital, in a higher rate of growth of output (equation [9]). This increase in the growth rate is permanent. Trade liberalization is tantamount to a technological innovation that increases the output that can be produced from given inputs. In Solow's (1956) neoclassical growth model, freer trade increases the rate of growth of output temporarily as the economy moves from one steady-state growth path to another, higher, parallel path. The adjustment process may take a long time, but economic growth is ultimately exogenously determined and, therefore, unaffected by increased trade. In Romer's model, freer trade increases the growth rate of output permanently, as we have seen.[4] Thus, agricultural-trade liberalization, like trade liberalization in general, will increase the level and growth of total output over time, even though output may decrease in the short run because of the time it takes for former farmers, farm workers, and middlemen to learn new skills and to find profitable employment outside agriculture.

How large are the potential dynamic output gains from freer trade? Suppose that farm protection is reduced to one-fourth of its current level, from 80 percent to 20 percent. Such liberalization by 75 percent lowers the ratio of domestic to world market prices from 1.8 to 1.2, decreasing the distortion from 0.44 to 0.17. This could increase the level of total output gradually by about 2.4 percent in the EU once and for all, that is, by the difference between the starred estimate of a

[4] Specifically, the mechanisms that prevented increased efficiency and increased saving from stimulating growth permanently in the models of Harrod, Domar, and Solow are absent here because the production function (equation [8]) exhibits constant returns to capital. Because the adjustment may take a long time, however, the Solow model may be difficult to distinguish empirically from the Harrod-Domar-Romer version of the endogenous growth model employed in the text. The result that trade reform stimulates economic growth can thus be viewed either as a long-run property of endogenous growth or as a medium-term attribute of exogenous growth.

static output gain of 2.8 percent in Table 5 and the estimate of 0.4 percent above it in the table. Hence, if the efficiency index E is 0.33 before liberalization (corresponding to a capital-to-output ratio of 3), it will be 0.338 after liberalization. At higher price elasticities, the potential static output and efficiency gains will be even larger.

In the EFTA countries, and especially in Finland and Norway, where current farm support is highest relative to GDP,[5] the static output gains from reducing agricultural protection by 75 percent could be higher than in the EU, perhaps in the neighborhood of 3 percent of GDP or more.

Assuming a saving rate of, say, 20 percent of total output, the liberalization of farm trade by 75 percent could be expected to increase the rate of growth of total per capita output by 0.2 percent (equation [9]), other things being equal (see the starred entry in Table 6). That would mean a per capita increase in economic growth of about one-tenth under normal circumstances (from 2.0 percent to 2.2 percent per year, for example). Higher saving and investment rates, larger price elasticities, and more ambitious liberalization could produce even greater growth effects. If these numbers are indicative of the results that would emerge from detailed empirical case studies of the consequences of agricultural-trade liberalization, it seems reasonable to conclude that continued trade restrictions may be expensive indeed—provided that the slump in output during the adjustment period is not too deep and long.

Macroeconomic Aspects of Agriculture

The potential macroeconomic gains from agricultural-trade liberalization reviewed above bring farm problems and policies inevitably into the sphere of macroeconomic policy.

This is obvious as far as fiscal affairs are concerned. Persistent government budget deficits and the associated accumulation of public debt have been a major macroeconomic concern in many European countries for years. With agriculture absorbing about 70 percent of the EU's budget in recent years, it is clear that the governments of Europe could better come to grips with their fiscal problems if they could reduce expenditures on agricultural transfers. Moreover, by lowering food prices and thus increasing the purchasing power of households, farm-trade liberalization in Europe would create the occasion for either reducing government spending on social services or increasing taxation

[5] Iceland, also an EFTA member, is higher but has not yet reported the full cost of its farm protection to the OECD.

TABLE 6

DYNAMIC OUTPUT GAINS FROM AGRICULTURAL-TRADE LIBERALIZATION AS A FUNCTION OF THE SAVING RATE AND THE EFFICIENCY OF CAPITAL

(in percent)

Efficiency of Capital	Percent Liberalization	Saving Rate 0.15	0.20	0.25
0.334	37	0.1	0.1	0.1
0.338	75	0.1	0.2*	0.2
0.339	100	0.1	0.2	0.2

SOURCE: Author's computations based on equation (9).

or both. Farm-policy reform would therefore strengthen the fiscal position of European governments.

Agriculture, money, and exchange rates. The public-finance argument can be extended to the field of monetary affairs and inflation control. Consider a government that is confronted by the real or imagined need to devalue the national currency to strengthen the competitiveness of its export- and import-competing industries and bolster the balance of payments but that is reluctant to do so for fear of increased inflation. The Nordic countries, among others, have found themselves in this predicament repeatedly over the years (see Box 2). Suppose, further, that it would be difficult for the government to accompany the devaluation by fiscal and monetary restraint, because public-spending cuts are unpalatable and taxes and interest rates are deemed to be too high already. What can it do?

One way out of the dilemma is to boost aggregate supply by, yes, liberalizing farm trade. The resulting decrease in food prices can offset the inflationary effect of devaluation on domestic consumer prices and, hence, on wages. It is therefore possible in principle to devalue the currency if urgent need arises without generating a spiral of price and wage increases. The decline in the purchasing power of households through devaluation is then offset by increased purchasing power through a more efficient allocation of resources and lower prices. Put differently, freer trade drives a wedge between the wage earnings of households and the wage costs of enterprises. Unlike devaluation, lower food prices through increased competition and lower tariffs strengthen the purchasing power of households without adding to the wage costs of firms. In some cases, therefore, farm-policy reform can conceivably even be a substitute for, rather than a complement to, devaluation.

BOX 2

DEVALUATION WITHOUT INFLATION: AN EXAMPLE FROM ICELAND

Iceland has experienced more inflation since the 1950s than any other OECD country except Turkey. From 1955 to 1993, consumer prices in Iceland increased, on average, by 23 percent a year. A lax exchange-rate policy during most of this period played an important part in this development. A typical devaluation cycle began with a downswing in the fisheries—which account for more than half of export earnings—followed by pressure on the government to devalue the króna to restore profitability to the fishing industry. Without adequate monetary, fiscal, and financial restraint to contain inflation, repeated devaluations then fuelled a persistent wage-price spiral. This pattern was not broken until 1992, and then perhaps only temporarily. Even so, the real exchange rate remains too high for the Icelandic economy to be able to break loose from its excessive dependence on fish by developing a profitable, viable, and broadly based export industry. Icelandic exports have been stagnant at about one-third of GDP since the early 1970s, while the share of world exports in world output has increased by one-half. The authorities are reluctant to devalue the króna further mainly because they fear this would trigger a new wave of inflation.

Inflation could be averted, however, by accompanying the necessary devaluation with structural change: by imposing fishing fees on boat owners to encourage an efficient and fair reduction of a fishing fleet that has grown much too large in view of the maximum allowable catch (Gylfason, 1992), and, yes, by liberalizing agriculture. Imports comprise about 40 percent of consumer expenditure. A 10 percent devaluation, therefore, would need to be accompanied by a 7 percent decrease in domestic prices for the consumer price index and the purchasing power of wages to remain unchanged. This could be done by reducing domestic food prices by 27 percent (that is, from 400 percent to a little less than 300 percent of world market prices on average), because food accounts for about one-fourth of consumer expenditure on domestically produced goods and services. A more comprehensive liberalization of agriculture leading to, say, a 50 percent reduction of domestic food prices (from 400 percent to 200 percent of world prices) would similarly create scope for a 20 percent devaluation or thereabouts without inflation, other things being equal. Exports could then take off without a need to restrain domestic expenditure commensurately to keep inflation in check.

Consider next a central bank that faces loud demands for lower interest rates in order to stimulate the economy but hesitates to respond for fear of increased inflation. The governor can then say: "There is a better way. Let us, rather, bring food prices down through farm-trade reform. Then consumer prices, or at least inflation, will come down, and interest rates will follow. Let us, in other words, increase the real money supply by deflating prices through structural supply-side reforms in agriculture and elsewhere without increasing the money supply in circulation, thus bringing interest rates down without igniting inflation. Through this channel, the price level can be lowered without reducing the quantity of money."

This is why agricultural policies, and structural reforms in general, including labor-market reforms, belong on the agenda of central banks and, by implication, the International Monetary Fund (IMF). It must be noted, however, that these are all one-time options. Once done, they cannot be repeated.

Some numbers may throw light on the magnitudes involved. Roughly one-sixth of the average household budget in the EU is spent on food, mostly food produced in Europe. If food prices in Europe were to fall by one-third (say, from 1.8 to 1.2) and world market prices were to rise by one-fifth (say, from 1.0 to 1.2), thus eliminating the current 80 percent discrepancy between domestic and world market prices, then consumer prices in Europe could fall by almost 6 percent, other things being equal. The real money supply, purchasing power, and, ultimately, employment would rise correspondingly. Alternatively, a partial liberalization by 37 percent could lower food prices by 17 percent and consumer prices by 3 percent. In either case, with exchange rates floating against the rest of the world, European interest rates would probably fall by enough to stimulate investment at home and to strengthen the response of employment and output.

This prescription for aggregate-supply management is most plainly derived from a purely neoclassical framework, in which aggregate supply is independent of price and aggregate demand is inversely related to the price level in accordance with the quantity theory of money (see Figure 5). Farm-trade reform will probably bear fruit more slowly than monetary operations will because money can be issued more quickly than prices can be reduced in rigid markets. The effects of farm-trade reform, however, will most likely last longer. Moreover, unlike monetary expansion, aggregate-supply stimulus through trade reform is compatible with stable prices. The same argument applies to labor-market rigidities; their removal would lower production costs, prices, and interest rates and thus gradually increase employment, output, and investment.

One other point needs to be reiterated in this context. Because an overprotected, inefficient agricultural sector imposes unnecessarily high food prices on consumers and thus restrains their purchasing power, it depresses the demand for labor as well. This is another way of saying

FIGURE 5

HOW TRADE LIBERALIZATION RAISES OUTPUT AND LOWERS PRICES

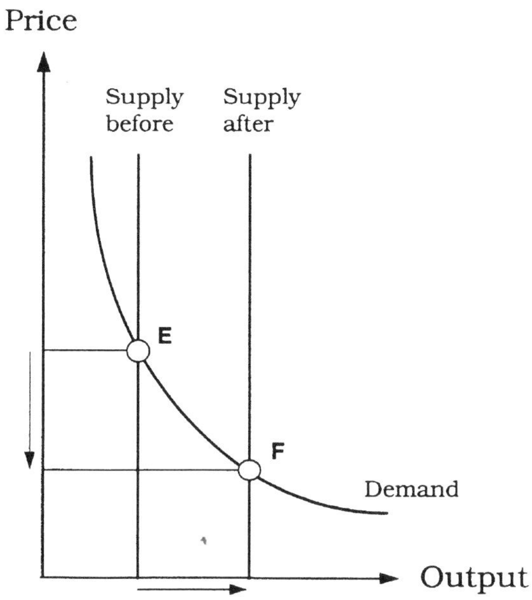

that trade reform is equivalent to technological progress in that it allows more output to be produced by given inputs (equation [8]). Despite the transitional increase in unemployment that can be expected from farm-trade liberalization (as occurred in New Zealand, for example), such reform will release new purchasing power, which will ultimately stimulate aggregate demand for goods and services and reduce joblessness. The high and persistent unemployment in Europe since the late 1970s increases the urgency of agricultural-policy reform.

Econometric estimates of the macroeconomic effects of dismantling the CAP seem to support this link. According to the OECD (1988), consumer prices would decline by almost 2 percent in response to lower agricultural prices, total employment would increase by almost 6 percent (while agricultural employment dropped by nearly 12 percent), and total output would rise by almost 4 percent (while agricultural production dropped by nearly 6 percent). These results abstract from delays and adjustment costs.

Finally, the link between exchange rates and the CAP should be considered. The CAP revolves around an elaborate system of variable levies and subsidies intended to maintain not only high but also uniform agricultural prices throughout the EU in order to avoid trade distortions. Because of this, it was considered necessary to shield the system from exchange-rate fluctuations. This was done by adjusting administered prices in inverse proportion to exchange-rate changes against the European currency unit (ecu), the unit of account in agricultural pricing. Farmers in countries the currencies of which had appreciated, however, were understandably reluctant to reduce their prices to conform to a common price level. Moreover, because domestic and foreign food products are close substitutes, devaluation tended to increase farm prices at home more fully and more quickly than it increased prices on many other goods. This produced resistance to the full adjustment of food prices to exchange rates and led to the establishment of an elaborate mechanism of Monetary Compensatory Amounts (MCAs) intended to accommodate price differences among member countries and thus to prevent trade distortions (Rosenblatt et al., 1988).

Under the European Monetary System (EMS), the pressure on farm prices and compensatory payments has been reduced. This is not to say that the CAP per se necessitates fixed exchange rates or a common currency in Europe. Yet a radical liberalization of the CAP would remove an important constraint on the EU's choice between fixed and flexible exchange rates in the future should the EU's current plan for a common currency fail.

Central and Eastern Europe. The EU now faces an important opportunity and challenge to bring the Central and Eastern European countries into the mainstream of European affairs. It would be unfortunate if, at this crucial juncture, Central and Eastern Europe were deprived of a chance to grow and prosper through increased exports. The expansion of trade is a prerequisite for necessary domestic restructuring and rapid growth, and possibly also for lasting political stability in the region. Therefore, the EU and EFTA countries must open their borders to increased trade with Central and Eastern Europe, not only in manufactured goods, but also in farm commodities and services. Agriculture is especially important in this regard, for three main reasons.

First, in view of the early history of the Central and Eastern European countries as important exporters of agricultural goods and of the notorious inefficiency of their agriculture under central planning, these countries can be expected to increase their farm outputs substantially in the years ahead (Hamilton and Winters, 1992). Agriculture remains relatively more important in Central and Eastern Europe than in Western Europe, accounting for about 10 to 20 percent of GDP and up to 30 percent of employment (World Bank, 1993). The contribution of agriculture to trade is also considerably larger in Eastern Europe than in the West. In 1989, farm exports averaged 11 percent of total merchandise exports from Central and Eastern Europe, ranging from 3 percent for Albania to 23 percent for Hungary (Anderson, 1991). A take-off of export-led growth in Central and Eastern Europe therefore requires farm-import liberalization in Western Europe, and thus a reorganization of the CAP far beyond the reforms of May 1992.

Second, without adequate market access for the farm goods in which they have a natural and historical comparative advantage, the Central and Eastern European countries may be led to embark on a premature and excessive reindustrialization that may strain their already severely polluted environments. (The role of agriculture will gradually diminish in any case as their economies develop, as it did in Western Europe.)

Third, the additional cost imposed by the entry of the Central and Eastern European countries into the EU in the first or second decade of the twenty-first century, or perhaps even sooner, would almost surely bankrupt the CAP in its present form (CEPR, 1992).

The integration of the Central and Eastern European countries into the mainstream of the European economy, and ultimately into the EU, provides an independent and important justification for restructuring the CAP (Josling, 1979). Political leaders must confront special interests at home by replacing aid with trade for the benefit of Europe as a whole. The potential gains from eliminating remaining inflation differentials and reducing inflation in Europe further through a common currency are certainly important, but they are probably not large compared with the gains from further liberalization of trade, especially agricultural trade. Farm-trade liberalization may well be one of the most effective and ultimately least expensive ways in which the OECD countries can promote economic reconstruction and development in Central and Eastern Europe.

Environmental protection. Because the natural environment is partly a public good, and because it involves substantial externalities, environmental preservation is a public concern. This consideration brings the maintenance and strengthening of rural communities within the purview of public policy, and it has sometimes been used as an argument for agricultural support.

According to Winters (1989/90) and Anderson (1992a, 1992b), however, farm protection has been counterproductive in this regard. First, by raising farm output and land prices, agricultural protection has encouraged intensive cultivation and construction in rural areas at the expense of both visual amenity and public access. Second, because it is widely and correctly perceived as unsustainable at present levels, agricultural support encourages the over-exploitation of land, with gradual soil erosion as a result; farmers will, in Winters' words, "make hay while the sun shines." Third, because farming is relatively capital and energy intensive, price support stimulates the use of chemical fertilizers and energy, including oil, and thus tends to increase pollution. On all three counts, therefore, lower prices of farm goods and of land following farm-trade liberalization seem more likely to preserve than to harm the environment. Insofar as farm policies are appropriate instruments of environmental protection, then, reducing price support seems the way to go.

The most efficient way of strengthening rural communities is not through farm support of any sort but through regional assistance that is not tied to specific activities. As noted by Johnson (1991, chap. 11), the populations of rural communities in Western Europe and North America have not declined with agriculture in this century, because most former farmers have found new jobs at or near home. Moreover, the gradual decline of employment in agriculture conceals substantial flows into and out of the farm labor force, in part presumably because generous farm support induces entry by new labor and capital into agriculture. This means that net migration of labor out of agriculture would be considerably more rapid under less extravagant farm policies, without gross migration from agriculture necessarily being affected.

Most important, however, it can be argued that education and human services in rural areas deserve public support on the grounds that the single most significant cause of low rural incomes is lack of schooling and skills (Johnson, 1991, chap. 12). Price support is not well suited to reducing income differentials resulting primarily from discrimination in educational opportunities. This is perhaps the most important reason why agricultural protection should, in part at least, be converted to improved education and infrastructure in rural areas, and why ministries of agriculture should perhaps be incorporated into ministries of education and culture to secure an equitable distribution of public support for education and culture among all communities.

Economic development. Before concluding, consideration must be given to the consequences of the CAP for developing countries, many of which rely on farm exports for much of their foreign-exchange earnings.

By restricting foreign access to European markets and by overproducing agricultural goods, the European nations depress food prices in world markets. According to the OECD (1987), a unilateral across-the-board reduction by 10 percent of the protection afforded by the CAP would increase the world market prices of most commodities by 0.6 percent (for sugar) to 2.9 percent (for milk). A complete liberalization of farm trade in Europe would raise world market prices by 5 percent (for wheat) to 28 percent (for dairy products), according to Koester and Valdés (1984). These results are based on partial-equilibrium models and thus probably understate the real effects.

Long-run general-equilibrium analysis yields higher estimates of the price and income effects of farm-trade liberalization on developing countries. If, for example, the industrial countries were to liberalize their farm policies enough to increase world market prices by 10 percent, the output gain to the developing countries would amount to between 1 and 2 percent of their GDP (Loo and Tower, 1989). This is not to say that the rest of the world would gain uniformly from a liberalization of the CAP; some countries would lose, including Japan, Korea, and Pakistan, for example. Several studies reviewed by the IMF (Rosenblatt et al., 1988) lead to similar conclusions. The IMF also reports empirical evidence that the CAP destabilizes world commodity prices substantially by insulating European markets from external commodity-price fluctuations without countercyclical stock management by the EU.

3 CONCLUSION

European agriculture is a macroeconomic concern. The cost of the CAP has been, and remains, huge. The average estimate of the total transfers from consumers and taxpayers to farmers and landowners through the CAP, extracted from empirical studies undertaken in the 1980s, suggests a gross cost of about 2 percent of European GDP and a deadweight loss equivalent to about 1 percent of GDP.

These figures are almost surely too low, however, because they are based on short-run partial-equilibrium analyses that do not reflect the long-run consequences of the implicit discrimination imposed by agricultural protection on other parts of the economy. When assessed by general-equilibrium techniques, the long-run gains from transferring labor, capital, and other resources from agriculture to industry, trade, and services, where productivity is higher, can easily reach 3 percent of GDP in the long run, with a corresponding reduction in joblessness over time insofar as it is caused by insufficient purchasing power. Furthermore, freer trade in farm products is likely to increase economic growth, possibly permanently.

In assessing the full cost of agricultural protection in Europe and elsewhere, it is thus important not only to include the welfare lost through price distortions, along the lines suggested by Harberger (as has been common in applied work), but also to consider the output foregone in the economy as a whole, in the tradition of Smith and Ricardo, and the dynamic growth effects, suggested by Harrod, Domar, Solow, and Romer. Moreover, one must also take into account the international ramifications of Europe's agricultural policy to arrive at a complete empirical assessment of its current cost.

D. Gale Johnson (1991, p. 230) hits the mark in his brilliant book *World Agriculture in Disarray*, where he writes:

> The fact that several studies done by different groups of researchers arrive at much larger negative effects of agricultural protection than had been derived from partial equilibrium studies requires that we revise the general view that the welfare or real income losses from protection are so small that they need to be given little weight. The questions raised by the new studies make it incumbent on policy-makers to give serious attention to reconsidering the potential gains and losses from agricultural protection. The potential losses in income and employment revealed by the recent studies

are large and should no longer be ignored in discussion of agricultural policies.

These potential gains and losses should also be considered in current debate of macroeconomic problems and policies in Europe. Extending the debate in this direction will not be easy, however. Resistance to farm reform, and even to rational debate about farm-policy issues, seems to be deeply rooted in national attitudes and sentiments. In many European farming families, the mere discussion of farm-policy reform is viewed as an attack upon their work and way of life. This is unfortunate, but feelings are facts, too. Even so, economists cannot permit their analyses and advice to be unduly restrained by political expediency or special interests.

APPENDIX A

Let the relation between domestic and world market prices be given by

$$\pi = (1 - c)\pi^* \ , \qquad \text{(A1)}$$

where π and π^* are the relative prices of industrial and agricultural goods at home and abroad and c is a constant that reflects the extent of the initial price distortion ($0 < c < 1$). Geometrically, the distortion parameter (c) reflects the angle between the two relative-price lines where they cross at point E in Figure 2 in the text. The distortion parameter (c) can also be expressed in terms of the tariff equivalent (t) of the farm-trade distortion as follows:

$$c = 1 - \frac{\pi}{\pi^*} = 1 - \frac{p_I\,[p_A(1 + t)]}{p_I p_A} = 1 - \frac{1}{1 + t} = \frac{t}{1 + t} \ ,$$

where p_I and p_A are the world market prices of industrial and agricultural goods. As the tariff equivalent (t) ranges from zero to infinity, the distortion parameter (c) spans the range from 0 to 1. Farm-trade liberalization reduces or eliminates the distortion, thus decreasing domestic agricultural prices relative to industrial ones, so that π increases to π^*.

National output is defined as the sum of industrial output (I) and agricultural output (A), measured in industrial goods:

$$Y = I + \left(\frac{p_A}{p_I}\right)A = 1 + \left(\frac{1}{\pi^*}\right)A \ . \qquad \text{(A2)}$$

The production-possibility frontier is described by the function

$$A = F(I) \ . \qquad \text{(A3)}$$

The first and second derivatives of F are both negative ($F' < 0$ and $F'' < 0$), indicating that both goods are produced under conditions of diminishing returns so that increasing costs of production prevail. This means that the production-possibility frontier is concave.

Profit maximization requires a tangency between the production-possibility frontier and the foreign relative-price line:

$$F'(I) = -\pi^* \tag{A4}$$

at the free-trade point F in the figure and, likewise, a tangency between the production-possibility frontier and the domestic relative-price line, $F'(I) = -\pi$, at the initial autarky point E.

The increase in industrial output (ΔI) from E to F is approximated by differentiating equation (A4) and solving for ΔI as a function of $\Delta\pi$, which equals $\pi^* - \pi = c\pi^*$ by equation (A1):

$$\Delta I = -F''^{-1}(I)(\pi^* - \pi) = F''^{-1}(I)c\pi^* \,. \tag{A5}$$

The approximate decrease in agricultural output (ΔA) is obtained by evaluating a second-order Taylor expansion of the production-possibility frontier in equation (A3) around point E in the figure:

$$\Delta A = F'(I)\Delta I - \frac{1}{2}F''(I)(\Delta I)^2 \,. \tag{A6}$$

The approximate increase in total output (ΔY) from E to F is found by substituting from equation (A6) into equation (A2) after taking first differences on both sides of the latter equation at given world market prices. This gives

$$\Delta Y = \Delta I + \left(\frac{1}{\pi^*}\right)\left[F'(I)\Delta I - \frac{1}{2}F''(I)(\Delta I)^2\right] = -\frac{1}{2\pi^*}F''(I)(\Delta I)^2 \tag{A7}$$

by using equation (A4). Squaring equation (A5) and substituting the result into equation (A7) yields the equation for output gain:

$$\Delta Y = mc^2 \,, \tag{A8}$$

where m denotes the multiple $\frac{1}{2}(F'/F'')$.

This is equation (3) in the text. The output gain from trade liberalization thus depends solely on the shape of the production-possibility frontier and the magnitude of the initial price distortion. The multiplicative factor can be expressed as $m = \frac{1}{2}(Ib)$, where $b = F'/(F''I)$ is the elasticity of industrial production with respect to its relative price.

Consider this production-possibility function, for example:

$$A = q\left(a - \frac{1}{1 + 1/b}I^{1+1/b}\right) \,, \tag{A9}$$

where q reflects productivity in agriculture and a and b are positive constants. The slope of the function at point F is

$$\frac{\partial A}{\partial I} = F'(I) = -qI^{1/b} = -\pi^* , \quad \text{(A10)}$$

so that

$$I = \left(\frac{\pi^*}{q}\right)^b . \quad \text{(A11)}$$

Hence, the price elasticity of industrial output is fixed at b anywhere on the frontier. The corresponding price elasticity of agricultural output, $(\partial A/\partial \pi^*)(\pi^*/A)$, equals $-b\pi^* I/A$ and varies inversely with the share of agriculture in total output.

The increase in industrial production as its relative price at home rises from π to π^* is found by differentiating equation (A11):

$$\Delta I = \left(\frac{1}{q}\right)^b b\pi^{*b-1}(\pi^* - \pi) = \left(\frac{\pi^*}{q}\right)^b b\pi^{*-1}c\pi^* = bcI . \quad \text{(A12)}$$

The corresponding decrease in domestic agricultural production follows from equations (A6), (A9), and (A12):

$$\Delta A = -qI^{1/b}\Delta I + \frac{1}{2b}qI^{(1/b)-1}(\Delta I)^2 = -qI^{1/b}bcI$$

$$+ \frac{1}{2b}qI^{(1/b)-1}b^2c^2I^2 . \quad \text{(A13)}$$

The resulting increase in total output is found by substituting from equations (A12) and (A13) into equation (A2):

$$\frac{g}{1+g} = \frac{1}{2}\left(\frac{I}{Y}\right)bc^2 . \quad \text{(A14)}$$

Here $g = \Delta Y/Y$ is the proportional increase in output from E to F in Figure 2 (with initial output as a base), I/Y is the share of industry (i.e., manufacturing, construction, trade, and services) in total output after the structural adjustment has been completed, and b is the elasticity of industrial production with respect to its relative price, $b = F'/(F''I)$, from equation (A11). If multiplied through by Y, equation (A14) becomes identical to equation (A8).

Equation (A14) has the following interpretation. The more severe the initial distortion (c), the larger the correction that will need to be made and, hence, the greater will be the gain in total output. The greater the elasticity of industrial production to its relative price (b), the greater will be the response of total output to trade reform. The more ambitious the structural adjustment undertaken, the larger will be the share of industry (I/Y) at the end of the day and, hence, again, the greater will be the gain in total output from agricultural-trade liberalization. This equation can be used to assess the potential strength of the empirical link between trade liberalization and the ensuing expansion of total output (g) in general equilibrium for given estimates of I/Y, b, and c, as in the text (Gylfason, 1993).

Agricultural productivity, reflected by the parameter q above, has been assumed to remain unchanged thus far. Assume now that farm productivity increases when agricultural trade is liberalized, according to

$$\frac{\Delta q}{q} = kc \ , \tag{A15}$$

where k is a positive constant. The greater the initial farm-trade distortion (c), the greater will be the resulting proportional increase in agricultural productivity. By similar arithmetic as that above, total output can be shown to increase further with increased farm productivity, as follows:

$$\frac{g}{1+g} = \frac{1}{2}\left(\frac{I}{Y}\right) b \left(\frac{\Delta q}{q}\right)^2 . \tag{A16}$$

This equation describes the expansion of output by NQ from point F to point G in Figure 3, whereas equation (A14) describes the increase in output by MN from point E to point F in the figure. The total increase in output by MQ from E through F to G is found by adding equations (A14) and (A16) by using equation (A15):

$$\frac{g}{1+g} = \frac{1}{2}\left(\frac{I}{Y}\right) b\left(1 + k^2\right) c^2 . \tag{A17}$$

With this addition, the multiple m in equation (3) in the text equals $\frac{1}{2}(F'/F'')(1 + k^2)$ in general and $\frac{1}{2}bI(1 + k^2)$ in the example given above.

To take another example, consider an economy in which agriculture is characterized by decreasing returns to labor use, so that

$$A = q \ln(1 + L_A) \ , \tag{A18}$$

where $\ln(1 + L_A)$ is the natural logarithm of (1 *plus*) employment in agriculture. Let there be constant returns to labor use in industry:

$$I = hL_I \;, \tag{A19}$$

where L_I is employment in industry and the output-input coefficient (h) is a positive constant.

The exogenously given labor force (L) is fully employed in agriculture and industry:

$$L = L_A + L_I \;. \tag{A20}$$

Equations (A18), (A19), and (A20) imply the production-possibility frontier

$$A = q \ln\left(1 + L - \frac{I}{h}\right), \tag{A21}$$

with $F' = -q[h(1 + L) - I]^{-1} < 0$ and $F'' = -q[h(1 + L) - I]^{-2} < 0$, as required for concavity. The first-order condition for maximum profit is

$$\frac{\partial A}{\partial I} = F'(I) = -\frac{q}{h(1 + L) - I} = -\pi* \;, \tag{A22}$$

so that

$$I = h(1 + L) - \frac{q}{\pi*} \;. \tag{A23}$$

The reaction of industrial output to an increase in its relative price is therefore

$$\Delta I = \frac{q}{\pi*^2}(\pi* - \pi) = \frac{q}{\pi*^2}c\pi* = \frac{q}{\pi*}c \;. \tag{A24}$$

The corresponding price elasticity of industrial production is

$$\begin{aligned} b &= \frac{\partial I}{\partial \pi*}\,\frac{\pi*}{I} = \frac{q}{\pi*^2}\,\frac{\pi*}{I} = \frac{q}{\pi* I} = \frac{q[h(1 + L) - I]}{qI} \\ &= \frac{h(1 + L_A)}{I} \;. \end{aligned} \tag{A25}$$

The price elasticity of industrial output is not fixed here, as in the preceding example, but varies inversely with the output. The price elasticity of agricultural output is also variable and equals $-q/A$. The smaller and more productive the farm sector, the more responsive it is to price incentives.

The reaction of total output to an increase in the relative price of industrial output (that is, a decrease in the relative price of agricultural goods) can be found by substituting the above values of $F' = -q[h(1 + L) - I]^{-1}$ and $F'' = -q[h(1 + L) - I]^{-2}$ and the square of equation (A24) into equation (A8). This operation, with equation (A25), gives equation (A14), as before. Moreover, by adding technological progress on top of trade liberalization, using equation (A15), we again obtain equation (A17).

APPENDIX B

Let output be produced by labor (L) and capital (K) according to a Cobb-Douglas production function

$$Y = TL^{a}K^{1-a} , \tag{B1}$$

where a is the elasticity of output with respect to labor. The accumulated technological knowledge (T) is tied to the capital stock by

$$T = EK^{a(1-b)} , \tag{B2}$$

where E reflects efficiency and b is a constant (Romer, 1986, 1989). An expansion of the capital stock increases technological proficiency.

Employment is related to the capital stock by

$$L = K^{b} , \tag{B3}$$

with $0 < b < 1$. More capital requires more workers to operate it, but relatively fewer workers are needed as capital expands.

Given the constellation of exponents assumed in equations (B1), (B2), and (B3), output is proportional to the capital stock:

$$Y = EK . \tag{B4}$$

This Harrod-Domar-Romer type of linear aggregate production function with constant returns to capital conforms to the stylized facts behind Solow's neoclassical growth model. First, the capital-to-output ratio (K/Y) is constant in the long run for given E. Second, average labor productivity (Y/L) rises over time because $\Delta L/L = b\Delta K/K = b\Delta Y/Y < \Delta Y/Y$. Third, real wages ($w$) increase over time with productivity because $w = aY/L$. Fourth, real interest rates (i) are constant in the long run because $i = (1 - a)Y/K$. Fifth, wage income *plus* interest equals output ($wL + iK = Y$). None of these standard properties is violated by the constant-returns-to-capital production function (equation [B4]).

Suppose saving (S) is proportional to output ($S = rY$), where r is the saving rate. Further, suppose saving equals gross investment (V), which equals net investment *plus* depreciation ($V = \Delta K + nK$), where n is the depreciation rate. Then

$$S = rY = V = \Delta K + nK = \frac{\Delta Y}{E} + n\frac{Y}{E}, \tag{B5}$$

for given E by equation (B4). It then follows that

$$g = rE - n, \tag{B6}$$

where $g = \Delta Y/Y$ as before.

Increased efficiency (E) thus results not only in a higher level of output (equation [A14]), but also in a permanently higher rate of growth of output (equation [B6]).

REFERENCES

Anderson, Kym, "Agriculture's Role in Transforming Socialist Economies," Geneva, GATT Secretariat, and Adelaide, University of Adelaide, 1991, processed.

———, "Agricultural Trade Liberalisation and the Environment: A Global Perspective," *World Economy*, 15 (January 1992a), pp. 153-171.

———, "Effects on the Environment and Welfare of Liberalizing World Trade: The Cases of Coal and Food," chap. 8 in Kym Anderson and Richard Blackhurst, eds., *The Greening of World Trade Issues*, London, Harvester Wheatsheaf, and Ann Arbor, University of Michigan Press, 1992b.

———, "Multilateral Trade Negotiations, European Integration, and Farm Policy Reform," *Economic Policy*, 18 (April 1994), pp. 14-52.

Bale, Malcolm D., and Ernst Lutz, "Price Distortions in Agriculture and Their Effects: An International Comparison," *American Journal of Agricultural Economics*, 63 (February 1981), pp. 8-22.

Baumol, William J., and William G. Bowen, *Performing Arts—The Economic Dilemma*, New York, Twentieth Century Fund, 1966.

Bohlin, Olof, Per-Martin Meyersson, and Ingemar Ståhl, *Makten över maten. Livsmedelssektorns politiska ekonomi*, Stockholm, SNS, 1984 [Also available in English as *The Political Economy of Food Policy*, Stockholm, SNS, 1986].

Buckwell, Allan E., David R. Harvey, Kenneth J. Thomson, and Kevin A. Parton, *The Costs of the Common Agricultural Policy*, London and Canberra, Croom Helm, 1982.

Buckwell, Allan, and John Medland, "The Effects of Trade Liberalisation: Problems of Modelling the Effects of Liberalising Agricultural Trade," *European Economic Review*, 35, No. 2/3 (April 1991), pp. 552-561.

Bureau of Agricultural Economics (Australia), *Agricultural Policies in the European Community: Their Origins, Nature and Effects on Production and Trade*, Canberra, Government Publications Service, 1985.

Burniaux, Jean-Marc, and Jean Waelbroeck, "The Impact of CAP on Developing Countries: A General Equilibrium Analysis," in Christopher Stevens and Joan Verloren van Themaat, eds., *Pressure Groups, Policies, and Development: EEC and the Third World: A Survey 5*, London, Hodder and Stoughton, 1985.

Cecchini, Paolo, Michel Catinat, and Alexis Jacquemin, *The European Challenge, 1992: The Benefits of a Single Market*, Aldershot and Brookfield, Vt., Gower, 1988.

Centre for Economic Policy Research (CEPR), *Monitoring European*

Integration: Is Bigger Better? The Economics of EC Enlargement, Annual Report, London, Centre for Economic Policy Research, 1992.

Crocombe, Graham T., Michael J. Enright, and Michael E. Porter, *Upgrading New Zealand's Competitive Advantage*, Auckland and New York, Oxford University Press, 1991.

Demekas, Dimitrios G., Kasper Bartholdy, Sanjeev Gupta, Leslie Lipschitz, and Thomas Mayer, "The Effects of the Common Agricultural Policy of the European Community: A Survey of the Literature," *Journal of Common Market Studies*, 27 (December 1988), pp. 113-145.

Dicke, Hugo, Jürgen B. Donges, Egbert Gerken, and Grant Kirkpatrick, "The Economic Effects of Agricultural Policy in West Germany," *Weltwirtshaftliches Archiv*, 124, No. 2 (June 1988), pp. 301-321 [Reprinted as chap. 4 in Stoeckel, Vincent, and Cuthbertson, 1989].

Domar, Evsey D., "Expansion and Employment," *American Economic Review*, 37 (March 1947), pp. 34-55.

Gardner, Bruce L., "Changing Economic Perspectives on the Farm Problem," *Journal of Economic Literature*, 30 (March 1992), pp. 1-61.

Gulbrandsen, Odd, and Assar Lindbeck, *The Economics of the Agricultural Sector*, Stockholm, Almquist and Wicksell, 1973.

Gylfason, Thorvaldur, "The Pros and Cons of Fishing Fees: The Case of Iceland," *EFTA Bulletin* 33, No. 3/4 (August-December 1992), pp. 6-9.

———, "Output Gains from Economic Liberalization: A Simple Formula," chap. 4 in Laszlo Somogyi, ed., *The Political Economy of the Transition Process in Eastern Europe*, London, Edward Elgar, 1993.

Hamilton, Carl B., and L. Alan Winters, "Trade with Eastern Europe," *Economic Policy*, 14 (April 1992), pp. 78-116.

Harberger, Arnold C., "Using the Resources at Hand More Effectively," *American Economic Review*, 49 (May 1959), pp. 134-146 [Reprinted as chap. 5 in Harberger, 1974].

———, "Taxation, Resource Allocation, and Welfare," in *The Role of Direct and Indirect Taxes in the Federal Reserve System*, Princeton, N.J., Princeton University Press for the National Bureau of Economic Research and the Brookings Institution, 1964 [Reprinted as chap. 2 in Harberger, 1974].

———, *Taxation and Welfare*, Boston, Little, Brown, 1974.

Harrod, Roy F., *Towards a Dynamic Economics*, Macmillan, London, 1948.

Isachsen, Arne Jon, Carl B. Hamilton, and Thorvaldur Gylfason, *Understanding the Market Economy*, Oxford and New York, Oxford University Press, 1992.

Johnson, D. Gale, *World Agriculture in Disarray*, 2d ed., London, Macmillan for the Trade Policy Research Centre, 1991.

Josling, Timothy E., "Questions for Farm Policy in an Enlarged European Community," *World Economy*, 2 (September 1979), pp. 343-362.

Koester, Ulrich, "The Experience with Liberalization Policies: The Case of the Agricultural Sector," *European Economic Review*, 35, No. 2/3 (April 1991), pp. 562-570.

Koester, Ulrich, and Alberto Valdés, "Reform of the CAP: Impact on the Third World," *Food Policy*, 9 (May 1984), pp. 94-98.
Leibenstein, Harvey, "Allocative Efficiency vs. 'X-Efficiency,'" *American Economic Review*, 56 (June 1966), pp. 392-415.
Loo, Thomas M., and Edward Tower, "Agricultural Protectionism and the Less Developed Countries: The Relationship between Agricultural Prices, Debt Servicing, and the Need for Development Aid," chap. 2 in Stoeckel, Vincent, and Cuthbertson, 1989.
Martin, John P., Jean-Marc Burniaux, François Delorme, Ian Lienert, and Dominique van der Mensbrugghe, "Economy-wide Effects of Agricultural Policies in OECD Countries: Simulation Results with WALRAS," *OECD Economic Studies*, Special Issue 13 (Winter 1989/90), pp. 131-172.
Miller, Marcus H., and John E. Spencer, "The Static Economic Effects of the UK Joining the EEC: A General Equilibrium Approach," *Review of Economic Studies*, 44 (February 1977), pp. 71-93.
Mitchell, Brian R., *European Historical Statistics, 1750-1975*, 2d rev. ed., London, Macmillan, 1980.
Morris, C. N., "The Common Agricultural Policy," *Fiscal Studies*, 1 (March 1980), pp. 17-35.
Organisation for Economic Co-operation and Development (OECD), *National Policies and Agricultural Trade*, Paris, OECD, 1987.
———, *OECD Economic Studies*, Special Issue 13, (Winter, 1989/90).
———, *New Zealand*, OECD Economic Surveys, Paris, OECD, 1991.
———, *Agricultural Policies, Markets and Trade, Monitoring and Outlook*, Paris, OECD, 1988, 1992, 1993a
———, *Historical Statistics*, Paris, OECD, 1993b.
———, *National Accounts*, Paris, OECD, 1993c.
Otsuka, Keijiro, and Yujiro Hayami, "Goals and Consequences of Rice Policy in Japan, 1965-80," *American Journal of Agricultural Economics*, 67 (August 1985), pp. 529-538.
Radetzki, Marian, "Hard Coal in Europe: Perspectives on a Global Market Distortion," *OPEC Review*, (June 1994), pp. 223-244.
Romer, Paul, "Increasing Returns and Long-Run Growth," *Journal of Political Economy*, 94 (October 1986), pp. 1002-1037.
———, "Capital Accumulation in the Theory of Long-Run Growth," in Robert J. Barro, ed., *Modern Business Cycle Theory*, Cambridge, Mass., Harvard University Press, 1989.
Rosenblatt, Julius, Thomas Mayer, Kasper Bartholdy, Dimitrios Demekas, Sanjeev Gupta, and Leslie Lipschitz, *The Common Agricultural Policy of the European Community, Principles and Consequences*, Occasional Paper No. 62, Washington, D.C., International Monetary Fund, November 1988.
Schiff, Maurice, and Alberto Valdés, *The Plundering of Agriculture in Developing Countries*, Washington, D.C., World Bank, 1992.
Sharker, Rakhal, Karl Meilke, and Michael Hoy, "The Political Economy of

Systematic Government Intervention in Agriculture," *Canadian Journal of Agricultural Economics*, 41 (November 1993), pp. 289-309.
Solow, Robert M., "A Contribution to the Theory of Economic Growth," *Quarterly Journal of Economics*, 46 (February 1956), pp. 65-94.
Spencer, John, "The European Economic Community: General Equilibrium Computations and the Economic Implications of Membership," in John Piggott and John Whalley, eds., *New Developments in Applied General Equilibrium Analysis*, Cambridge and New York, Cambridge University Press, 1985.
Stoeckel, Andrew B., and Jens Breckling, "Some Economywide Effects of Agricultural Policies in the European Community: A General Equilibrium Study," chap. 3 in Stoeckel, Vincent, and Cuthbertson, 1989.
Stoeckel, Andrew B., David Vincent, and Sandy Cuthbertson, *Macroeconomic Consequences of Farm Support Policies*, Durham, N.C., and London, Duke University Press, 1989.
Thomson, Kenneth J., and David R. Harvey, "The Efficiency of the Common Agricultural Policy," *European Review of Agricultural Economics*, 8 (1981), pp. 57-83.
Throsby, David, "The Production and Consumption of the Arts: A View of Cultural Economics," *Journal of Economic Literature*, 32 (March 1994), pp. 1-29.
Tyers, Rodney, "International Impacts of Protection: Model Structure and Results for EC Agricultural Policy," *Journal of Policy Modeling*, 7 (Summer 1985), pp. 219-252.
Tyers, Rodney, and Kym Anderson, "Distortions in World Food Markets: A Quantitative Assessment," background paper prepared for the *World Development Report*, 1986a, processed.
———, "Global Interactions and Trade Liberalization in Agriculture," background paper prepared for the *World Development Report*, 1986b, processed.
———, "Liberalizing OECD Agricultural Policies in the Uruguay Round: Effects on Trade and Welfare," Working Papers in Trade and Development, No. 87/10, Canberra, Australian National University, 1987.
Vincent, David, "Domestic Effects of Agricultural Protection in Asian Countries with Special Reference to Korea," chap. 5 in Stoeckel, Vincent, and Cuthbertson, 1989a.
———, "Effects of Agricultural Protection in Japan: An Economywide Analysis,", chap. 6 in Stoeckel, Vincent, and Cuthbertson, 1989b.
Winters, L. Alan, "The Economic Consequences of Agricultural Support: A Survey," *OECD Economic Studies*, 9 (Autumn 1987), pp. 7-54.
———, "The So-Called "Non-Economic" Objectives of Agricultural Support," *OECD Economic Studies*, 13 (Winter 1989/90), pp. 237-266.
World Bank, *World Development Report*, Washington, D.C., World Bank, 1986 and 1993.

PUBLICATIONS OF THE INTERNATIONAL FINANCE SECTION

Notice to Contributors

The International Finance Section publishes papers in four series: ESSAYS IN INTERNATIONAL FINANCE, PRINCETON STUDIES IN INTERNATIONAL FINANCE, and SPECIAL PAPERS IN INTERNATIONAL ECONOMICS contain new work not published elsewhere. REPRINTS IN INTERNATIONAL FINANCE reproduce journal articles previously published by Princeton faculty members associated with the Section. The Section welcomes the submission of manuscripts for publication under the following guidelines:

ESSAYS are meant to disseminate new views about international financial matters and should be accessible to well-informed nonspecialists as well as to professional economists. Technical terms, tables, and charts should be used sparingly; mathematics should be avoided.

STUDIES are devoted to new research on international finance, with preference given to empirical work. They should be comparable in originality and technical proficiency to papers published in leading economic journals. They should be of medium length, longer than a journal article but shorter than a book.

SPECIAL PAPERS are surveys of research on particular topics and should be suitable for use in undergraduate courses. They may be concerned with international trade as well as international finance. They should also be of medium length.

Manuscripts should be submitted in triplicate, typed single sided and double spaced throughout on 8½ by 11 white bond paper. Publication can be expedited if manuscripts are computer keyboarded in WordPerfect 5.1 or a compatible program. Additional instructions and a style guide are available from the Section.

How to Obtain Publications

The Section's publications are distributed free of charge to college, university, and public libraries and to nongovernmental, nonprofit research institutions. Eligible institutions may ask to be placed on the Section's permanent mailing list.

Individuals and institutions not qualifying for free distribution may receive all publications for the calendar year for a subscription fee of $40.00. Late subscribers will receive all back issues for the year during which they subscribe. Subscribers should notify the Section promptly of any change in address, giving the old address as well as the new.

Publications may be ordered individually, with payment made in advance. ESSAYS and REPRINTS cost $8.00 each; STUDIES and SPECIAL PAPERS cost $11.00. An additional $1.25 should be sent for postage and handling within the United States, Canada, and Mexico; $1.50 should be added for surface delivery outside the region.

All payments must be made in U.S. dollars. Subscription fees and charges for single issues will be waived for organizations and individuals in countries where foreign-exchange regulations prohibit dollar payments.

Please address all correspondence, submissions, and orders to:

International Finance Section
Department of Economics, Fisher Hall
Princeton University
Princeton, New Jersey 08544-1021

List of Recent Publications

A complete list of publications may be obtained from the International Finance Section.

ESSAYS IN INTERNATIONAL FINANCE

161. Alexis Rieffel, *The Role of the Paris Club in Managing Debt Problems*. (December 1985)
162. Stephen E. Haynes, Michael M. Hutchison, and Raymond F. Mikesell, *Japanese Financial Policies and the U.S. Trade Deficit*. (April 1986)
163. Arminio Fraga, *German Reparations and Brazilian Debt: A Comparative Study*. (July 1986)
164. Jack M. Guttentag and Richard J. Herring, *Disaster Myopia in International Banking*. (September 1986)
165. Rudiger Dornbusch, *Inflation, Exchange Rates, and Stabilization*. (October 1986)
166. John Spraos, *IMF Conditionality: Ineffectual, Inefficient, Mistargeted*. (December 1986)
167. Rainer Stefano Masera, *An Increasing Role for the ECU: A Character in Search of a Script*. (June 1987)
168. Paul Mosley, *Conditionality as Bargaining Process: Structural-Adjustment Lending, 1980-86*. (October 1987)
169. Paul A. Volcker, Ralph C. Bryant, Leonhard Gleske, Gottfried Haberler, Alexandre Lamfalussy, Shijuro Ogata, Jesús Silva-Herzog, Ross M. Starr, James Tobin, and Robert Triffin, *International Monetary Cooperation: Essays in Honor of Henry C. Wallich*. (December 1987)
170. Shafiqul Islam, *The Dollar and the Policy-Performance-Confidence Mix*. (July 1988)
171. James M. Boughton, *The Monetary Approach to Exchange Rates: What Now Remains?* (October 1988)
172. Jack M. Guttentag and Richard M. Herring, *Accounting for Losses On Sovereign Debt: Implications for New Lending*. (May 1989)
173. Benjamin J. Cohen, *Developing-Country Debt: A Middle Way*. (May 1989)
174. Jeffrey D. Sachs, *New Approaches to the Latin American Debt Crisis*. (July 1989)
175. C. David Finch, *The IMF: The Record and the Prospect*. (September 1989)
176. Graham Bird, *Loan-Loss Provisions and Third-World Debt*. (November 1989)
177. Ronald Findlay, *The "Triangular Trade" and the Atlantic Economy of the Eighteenth Century: A Simple General-Equilibrium Model*. (March 1990)
178. Alberto Giovannini, *The Transition to European Monetary Union*. (November 1990)
179. Michael L. Mussa, *Exchange Rates in Theory and in Reality*. (December 1990)
180. Warren L. Coats, Jr., Reinhard W. Furstenberg, and Peter Isard, *The SDR System and the Issue of Resource Transfers*. (December 1990)
181. George S. Tavlas, *On the International Use of Currencies: The Case of the Deutsche Mark*. (March 1991)

182. Tommaso Padoa-Schioppa, ed., with Michael Emerson, Kumiharu Shigehara, and Richard Portes, *Europe After 1992: Three Essays*. (May 1991)
183. Michael Bruno, *High Inflation and the Nominal Anchors of an Open Economy*. (June 1991)
184. Jacques J. Polak, *The Changing Nature of IMF Conditionality*. (September 1991)
185. Ethan B. Kapstein, *Supervising International Banks: Origins and Implications of the Basle Accord*. (December 1991)
186. Alessandro Giustiniani, Francesco Papadia, and Daniela Porciani, *Growth and Catch-Up in Central and Eastern Europe: Macroeconomic Effects on Western Countries*. (April 1992)
187. Michele Fratianni, Jürgen von Hagen, and Christopher Waller, *The Maastricht Way to EMU*. (June 1992)
188. Pierre-Richard Agénor, *Parallel Currency Markets in Developing Countries: Theory, Evidence, and Policy Implications*. (November 1992)
189. Beatriz Armendariz de Aghion and John Williamson, *The G-7's Joint-and-Several Blunder*. (April 1993)
190. Paul Krugman, *What Do We Need to Know About the International Monetary System?* (July 1993)
191. Peter M. Garber and Michael G. Spencer, *The Dissolution of the Austro-Hungarian Empire: Lessons for Currency Reform*. (February 1994)
192. Raymond F. Mikesell, *The Bretton Woods Debates: A Memoir*. (March 1994)
193. Graham Bird, *Economic Assistance to Low-Income Countries: Should the Link be Resurrected?* (July 1994)
194. Lorenzo Bini-Smaghi, Tommaso Padoa-Schioppa, and Francesco Papadia, *The Transition to EMU in the Maastricht Treaty*. (November 1994)
195. Ariel Buira, *Reflections on the International Monetary System*. (January 1995)
196. Shinji Takagi, *From Recipient to Donor: Japan's Official Aid Flows, 1945 to 1990 and Beyond*. (March 1995)

PRINCETON STUDIES IN INTERNATIONAL FINANCE

57. Stephen S. Golub, *The Current-Account Balance and the Dollar: 1977-78 and 1983-84*. (October 1986)
58. John T. Cuddington, *Capital Flight: Estimates, Issues, and Explanations*. (December 1986)
59. Vincent P. Crawford, *International Lending, Long-Term Credit Relationships, and Dynamic Contract Theory*. (March 1987)
60. Thorvaldur Gylfason, *Credit Policy and Economic Activity in Developing Countries with IMF Stabilization Programs*. (August 1987)
61. Stephen A. Schuker, *American "Reparations" to Germany, 1919-33: Implications for the Third-World Debt Crisis*. (July 1988)
62. Steven B. Kamin, *Devaluation, External Balance, and Macroeconomic Performance: A Look at the Numbers*. (August 1988)
63. Jacob A. Frenkel and Assaf Razin, *Spending, Taxes, and Deficits: International-Intertemporal Approach*. (December 1988)
64. Jeffrey A. Frankel, *Obstacles to International Macroeconomic Policy Coordination*. (December 1988)

65. Peter Hooper and Catherine L. Mann, *The Emergence and Persistence of the U.S. External Imbalance, 1980-87.* (October 1989)
66. Helmut Reisen, *Public Debt, External Competitiveness, and Fiscal Discipline in Developing Countries.* (November 1989)
67. Victor Argy, Warwick McKibbin, and Eric Siegloff, *Exchange-Rate Regimes for a Small Economy in a Multi-Country World.* (December 1989)
68. Mark Gersovitz and Christina H. Paxson, *The Economies of Africa and the Prices of Their Exports.* (October 1990)
69. Felipe Larraín and Andrés Velasco, *Can Swaps Solve the Debt Crisis? Lessons from the Chilean Experience.* (November 1990)
70. Kaushik Basu, *The International Debt Problem, Credit Rationing and Loan Pushing: Theory and Experience.* (October 1991)
71. Daniel Gros and Alfred Steinherr, *Economic Reform in the Soviet Union: Pas de Deux between Disintegration and Macroeconomic Destabilization.* (November 1991)
72. George M. von Furstenberg and Joseph P. Daniels, *Economic Summit Declarations, 1975-1989: Examining the Written Record of International Cooperation.* (February 1992)
73. Ishac Diwan and Dani Rodrik, *External Debt, Adjustment, and Burden Sharing: A Unified Framework.* (November 1992)
74. Barry Eichengreen, *Should the Maastricht Treaty Be Saved?* (December 1992)
75. Adam Klug, *The German Buybacks, 1932-1939: A Cure for Overhang?* (November 1993)
76. Tamim Bayoumi and Barry Eichengreen, *One Money or Many? Analyzing the Prospects for Monetary Unification in Various Parts of the World.* (September 1994)
77. Edward E. Leamer, *The Heckscher-Ohlin Model in Theory and Practice.* (February 1995)
78. Thorvaldur Gylfason, *The Macroeconomics of European Agriculture.* (May 1995)

SPECIAL PAPERS IN INTERNATIONAL ECONOMICS

16. Elhanan Helpman, *Monopolistic Competition in Trade Theory.* (June 1990)
17. Richard Pomfret, *International Trade Policy with Imperfect Competition.* (August 1992)
18. Hali J. Edison, *The Effectiveness of Central-Bank Intervention: A Survey of the Literature After 1982.* (July 1993)

REPRINTS IN INTERNATIONAL FINANCE

26. Peter B. Kenen, *The Use of IMF Credit*; reprinted from *Pulling Together: The International Monetary Fund in a Multipolar World*, 1989. (December 1989)
27. Peter B. Kenen, *Transitional Arrangements for Trade and Payments Among the CMEA Countries*; reprinted from *International Monetary Fund Staff Papers* 38 (2), 1991. (July 1991)
28. Peter B. Kenen, *Ways to Reform Exchange-Rate Arrangements*; reprinted from *Bretton Woods: Looking to the Future*, 1994. (November 1994)